DVD Guitar Shred

Written by Mike Mueller, Chad Johnson & Barrett Tagliarino
Video Performer: Troy Stetina

ISBN-13: 978-1-4234-3309-5
ISBN-10: 1-4234-3309-2

HAL•LEONARD®
CORPORATION
7777 W. BLUEMOUND RD. P.O. BOX 13819 MILWAUKEE, WI 53213

Visit Hal Leonard Online at
www.halleonard.com

Table of Contents

Introduction

Ever since Eddie Van Halen and Yngwie Malmsteen turned the guitar-playing world upside-down in the late '70s and early '80s, guitarists everywhere have spent countless hours in the woodshed, working their fingers to the bone and wearing down frets in an effort to cop the fiery virtuosic licks of Joe Satriani, Steve Vai, Marty Friedman, and Paul Gilbert as well as Van Halen and Malmsteen.

If these kinds of monster chops have thus far eluded you, or if you've only recently discovered the world of terrifying technique, then *DVD Guitar Shred*, from Hal Leonard's exciting new At a Glance series, is your remedy. Not as "scholarly" or formal as traditional method books, the material in *DVD Guitar Shred* is presented in a snappy and fun manner intended to have you sweep picking, tapping, and otherwise shreddin' every which way but loose in virtually no time at all. Plus, the At a Glance series uses real songs by real artists to illustrate how the concepts you're learning are applied in some of the biggest hits of all time. For example, in *DVD Guitar Shred*, you'll learn licks from over 20 rock, shred, and instrumental classics, including Van Halen's "Eruption," White Lion's "Wait," Megadeth's "Hangar 18," and Yngwie Malmsteen's "Black Star."

Additionally, each book in the At a Glance series comes with a DVD containing video lessons that correspond to the printed material. The DVD that accompanies this book contains four video lessons, each approximately 8 to 10 minutes in length, that correspond to each chapter in *DVD Guitar Shred*. In these videos, acclaimed shred instructor Troy Stetina will show you in great detail everything from proper sweep picking technique to navigating long legato sequences without extraneous string noise.

As you work through *DVD Guitar Shred*, try to play the examples first on your own, and then check out the DVD for additional tips, or to see how a particular lick is executed. As the saying goes, "A picture is worth a thousand words," so be sure to use this invaluable tool on your quest to becoming the consummate shred guitarist.

Building Speed

Guitarists such as Yngwie Malmsteen, Paul Gilbert, and Steve Vai are all well known for their fretboard prowess, and their music likely has much to do with you purchasing and using this book. But skillful use of speed is not limited to the so-called "shred" genre. Indeed, more mainstream songs like Whitesnake's "Here I Go Again," Toto's "Rosanna," Dire Straits' "Sultans of Swing," and even Journey's "Faithfully" all feature magically melodic solos capped or injected with speedy lines that build to a musical climax. Further, they each serve as an example of why, even if speed is not really your focus as a player, it's a spine-tingling skill worth adding to your arsenal.

In this lesson, we're going to show you some basic speed-building exercises for both picking and legato sequences in rock lead-guitar styles to help you build monster chops regardless of your musical style. It's important, though, that you realize and understand that speed alone is just speed. The exercises presented in this chapter will also improve the tone you produce with your hands as well as your ability to keep tempo and thus stay in the groove.

Using a Metronome

Ever notice how the lines of some technically gifted guitarists, like John Petrucci, Al Di Meola, or Paul Gilbert, are so precise and in the groove? That's because they're all proponents of practicing with a metronome—the essential tool for keeping tempo steady while you develop accuracy and gradually work up your speed. If you try to play fast before you can play slowly, accurately, and with solid time, you'll just get sloppy results.

If you've already got one and know how to use it, skip ahead to the first exercise, set a tempo at which you can play it perfectly, and go. If you don't own a metronome, stop reading, get to a music store, and buy one! If you own one but aren't familiar with how it works, read on.

First, set your metronome to a tempo at which you can play a scale up and down, using alternate picking and an eighth-note rhythm (two notes per metronome click), without making any mistakes. Playing straight scales isn't the most musical endeavor but it will help you memorize the scale's shape and sound while building your alternate picking technique and timing. If you're not sure what tempo to start with, try 72 bpm.

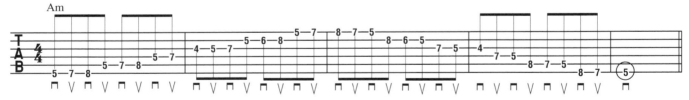

OK, let's try it with an A minor scale in fifth position.

How to Practice

Before you begin the exercises, we want to spend some time talking about *practice*. As we mentioned, you should be using alternate picking for all of the exercises and sequences in this lesson. Besides playing to a metronome, you should tap your foot in time with it. This will help you internalize the groove and feel for playing in solid time.

Once you've achieved a basic familiarity with whichever scale or exercise you're working on, write down the tempo at which you could play it cleanly with the metronome. Start off slowly every day, and inch the metronome up to the highest point you had it the day before, if possible. On some days it will be slower than before. This is normal.

Near the end of your practice session, try bumping it up one notch higher, just to see where the ceiling is. Don't repeatedly attempt to play at a tempo beyond your reach, as this will only teach you bad habits like playing with too much tension in your hands, arms, or body. Stay relaxed, and take your time building up your speed.

OK, let's play through another scale, this time A major, to help you warm up. Remember, start slowly and concentrate on the finger pattern and your pick attack rather than speed.

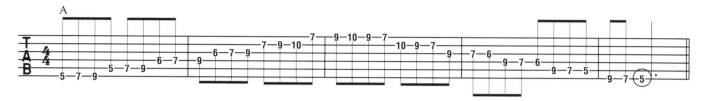

Try playing both the A minor and A major scale patterns in other keys, too, moving them up and down the neck so that you become accustomed to how your fingers feel with the different fret widths.

Scale Sequences

Playing scales makes for a great warm-up, and it certainly helps build your technique, but like we said, it's not the most musically applicable exercise around. To better build speed and technique with "real-life" musical phrases, we use melodic fragments called *scale sequences* to navigate the scale. These sequences are quite useful for building speed and coordination.

The first exercise is built using a four-note sequence from the A minor scale, resulting in note groupings of A–B–C–D, B–C–D–E, C–D–E–F, and so on, until we reach the highest note of the scale pattern—the high C at the eighth fret on the first string. Then you reverse the sequence and descend the scale.

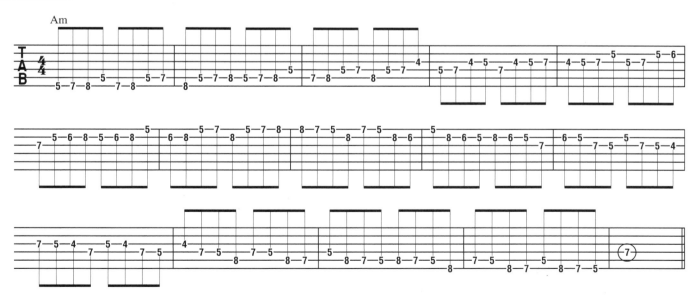

Here's the same scale sequence, only this time in A major.

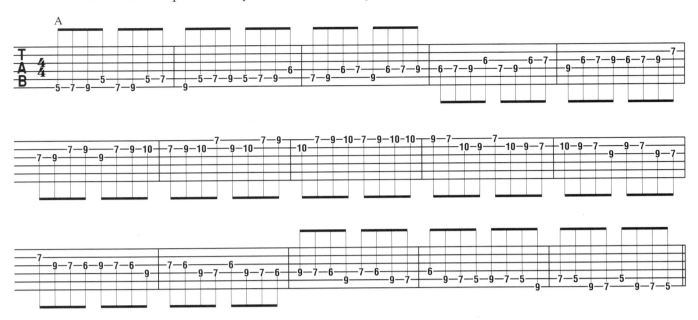

Pentatonic Sequences

The major and minor scales you've been using are primarily three-notes-per-string shapes. This physical layout results in certain pick attack patterns that can become crutches when you play fast lines. But to become a true fretboard master, you need to feel comfortable with any scale shape or pattern. One of the easiest ways to throw your budding speed chops a curveball is to toss in the two-notes-per-string minor pentatonic box shape. And because nearly all rock guitarists use sequences from the minor pentatonic scale, it's an incredibly functional exercise as well.

To kick things off, let's check out some sequences within the A minor pentatonic scale in fifth position. The first sequence is constructed with a groups-of-three pattern in which we'll play all three notes within one beat—a triplet rhythm. Make sure your foot is tapping with the metronome as always, but now you'll alternate-pick three notes per click. If you need to slow the tempo down to do this, that's fine. It's more important right now to play it cleanly than quickly. Also, you'll notice that every other three-note sequence will begin with an upstroke, which will further improve your speed skills.

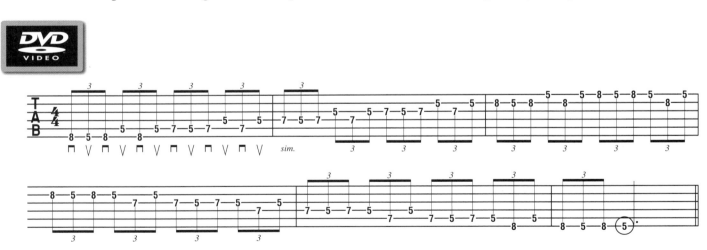

This next pentatonic sequence is a favorite of guitarists Zakk Wylde, Eric Johnson, and Joe Bonamassa—particularly the descending portion of it. Arranged in groups of six and notated as sextuplets (six sixteenth notes per beat), the sequence is played with a straight feel rather than with a triplet feel, as is common with sextuplets. Also, because you're squeezing six notes into each metronome click, you'll need to start at a slow tempo; try beginning at 40 bpm. Trust me, it's not as slow as it sounds!

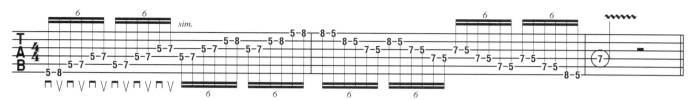

For this next pentatonic sequence, we shift back to an eighth-note rhythm, but we're now using an eight-note grouping. This one is actually very similar to the previous six-note grouping, except that you descend the minor pentatonic scale by two notes at the end of each measure, to set up the next ascent.

Set your metronome at a comfortable tempo and don't forget to tap your foot as you play through the sequence.

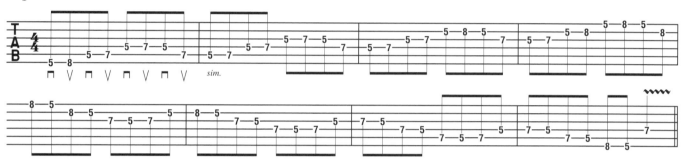

OK, let's raise the technical bar a little. In this next exercise, you'll ascend and descend the A minor pentatonic scale in a four-note sequence, skipping a string between the second and third notes of each grouping. This one is admittedly more methodical than musical, but the ability to accurately skip strings while staying in time is key to effective phrasing when playing high-speed lines.

To hear minor pentatonic scale sequences in action, check out Tony Iommi's solo in Black Sabbath's classic anthem "Children of the Grave." Notice how he includes the ♭5 blue note (B♭), which offsets the rhythm of the sequence for an interesting effect.

"CHILDREN OF THE GRAVE"
Black Sabbath

Words and Music by Frank Iommi, William Ward, John Osbourne and Terence Butler

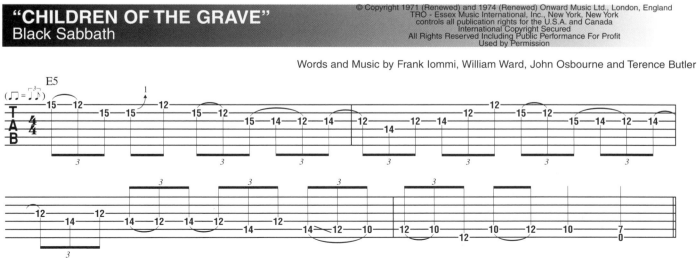

Legato Speed Building

Picking every single note of every speedy passage—especially a long one—can lead to what's best described as "typewriter" phrasing. To remedy this, guitarists can use *legato* techniques like hammer-ons, pull-offs, and slides to assume part of the work done by the picking hand, with the added benefit of making some phrases faster than we could alternate-pick them.

That being said, a common pitfall among guitarists using legato techniques in fast-paced lines is to rush through the legato parts simply because it's a little easier to execute. So as you play through the exercises and sequences in this section, try to evenly space all notes, focusing on the click of the metronome and the tap of your foot.

The first example is a rock lick based on the A Dorian mode. Here, focus on keeping steady time at the spot where a hammer-on is followed by two consecutive pull-offs in beats 2 and 3. Again, practice slowly and steadily, and keep your foot tapping with the metronome.

This next lick is one of Eddie Van Halen's favorite moves, where he alternates hammer-ons and picked notes, from string to string. Take note here of the fingering pattern, also one of Van Halen's creations, which has come to be known as the "EVH" scale. Because of its harmonic ambiguity, it's not often used in the context of melodic contour but rather as a vehicle for fast passages connecting point A to point B within a solo.

The alternation of picked and legato triplet groupings will really test your ability to stay in tempo. Start slowly enough that you don't rush the legato portions.

Legato Sequences

To further round out your speed-building regimen, you can go back and practice all of the scales and sequences you've learned so far using hammer-ons and pull-offs exclusively, picking only when a string comes into play for the first time for maximum efficiency.

For example, here's how the A minor pentatonic "groups of three" sequence sounds using this approach.

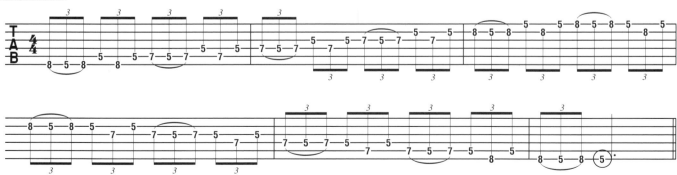

Now go back and try this approach on the A minor and A major scale patterns and sequences from this lesson.

More Sequences

To close out our speed-building lesson, here are a few patterns popular among shred guitarists. Be sure to play each sequence with both alternate picking and legato techniques, and move them up and down the fretboard. You can also, where possible, apply Eddie Van Halen's alternating picking and legato sequencing.

This first sequence is a major scale sequence in six-note groupings. To really drive home the rhythm, accent (>) the first note of each sequence. You can also experiment using a slight palm mute.

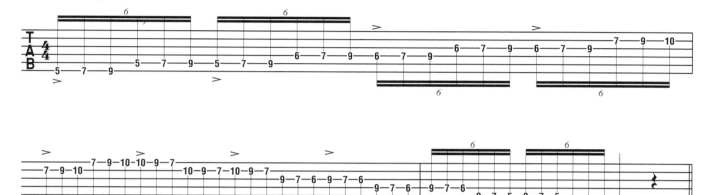

This next sequence—one of Paul Gilbert's favorites—groups the first six notes of the A minor scale together and moves them up one octave at a time. The new challenge here is making the position shifts while staying in time.

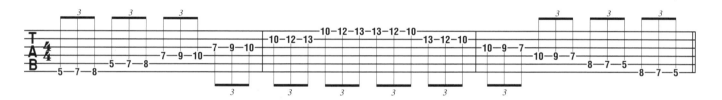

And finally, here is a Paul Gilbert–inspired major-scale sequence (starting on the 3rd) that ascends six notes, drops back one scale degree, and then ascends another six notes, drops back one scale degree, and so on and so on. Additionally, every six-note grouping begins in a new position, so you're continually shifting linearly up the fretboard.

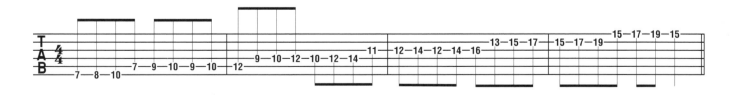

With his extremely unique approach to phrasing, Steve Vai doesn't often make use of sequences. When he does, however, he makes them count. This blazing lick, from "I Would Love To," sequences an arpeggio motive from G major down through each string set.

By Steve Vai

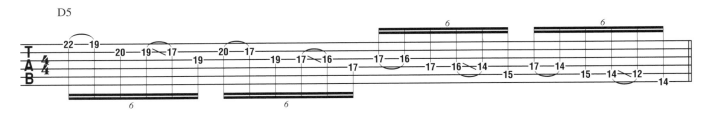

One of the more famous sequences in the shred world is Yngwie Malmsteen's neoclassical A harmonic minor lick that kicks off his solo in "I'll See the Light Tonight." This one shifts positions quickly and often, with no mercy. Strive for an even attack and make sure you stick to that metronome!

"I'LL SEE THE LIGHT TONIGHT"
Yngwie Malmsteen

Words and Music by Yngwie Malmsteen and Jeff Scott Soto

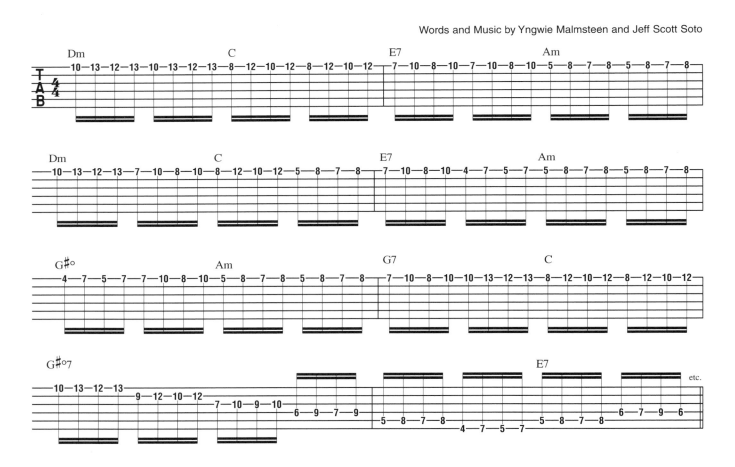

Legato Techniques

Listen to such master guitarists as Joe Satriani, Steve Vai, or Allan Holdsworth, and from time to time you'll hear long, liquid lines, like those you'd hear from a saxophonist, flowing freely from their fingers to create cascading torrents of notes. To generate that silky sound, they use the *legato* techniques. In Lesson 1, you used legato techniques in context of speed-building exercises, but here, we're going to further examine this essential shred technique.

From the Italian, meaning "smooth," legato techniques have been used by those and many other guitarists not only to execute fluid lines but also to facilitate blazing speed. As guitarists, we achieve a legato sound primarily with three techniques: *hammer-ons*, *pull-offs*, and *slides*.

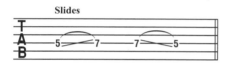

Those are the basic elements of the legato technique, and ones you're likely quite comfortable using. Yet it's interesting how many guitarists don't feel the need to practice legato playing after they get those basic moves down. They figure, "If I can pick every note of a lick, then I can surely play it with hammer-ons and pull-offs." But this is definitely not the case.

Sure, we all know lots of cliché licks that use some hammer-ons and pull-offs like these:

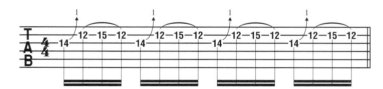
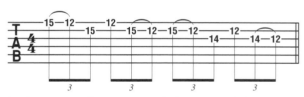

But not nearly as many players have true command over the legato technique, and that's exactly why we're here.

Exercises

Let's start with a few exercises that'll let you know right away where your legato technique stands.

First, if you're not familiar with the old 1-2-3-4 picking exercise, here it is.

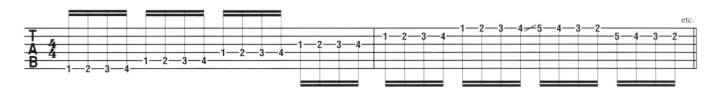

For this legato lesson, however, we're going to add a few twists. First, you start the four-note grouping on a different finger each time; and second, you only pick once for each string. When you reach beat 3 of bar 2, shift your fret hand up one fret and descend the pattern. When you reach the last note on the sixth string, move your hand up one more fret and continue repeating this process until you reach the twelfth fret.

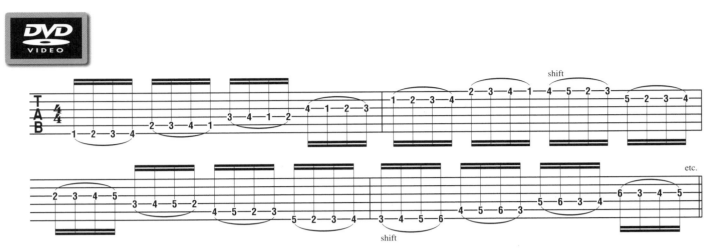

The next exercise is a three-note, triplet variation of the previous one. At first glance, this appears easier than the last one—*except* that you'll be using your fret hand's middle, ring, and pinky fingers to play it, rather than the stronger index, middle, and ring finger combination.

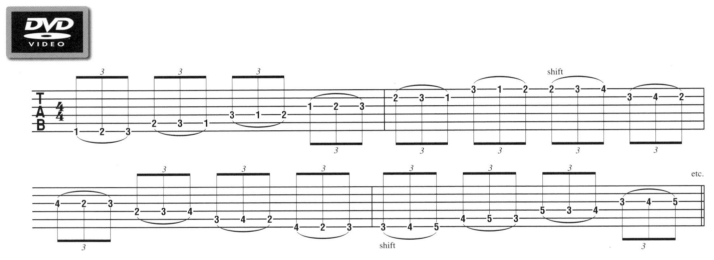

Right about now, you may be feeling a bit of animus toward us; that's OK, because we realize that someday when you're able to effortlessly pull off those Satriani-style legato runs, you'll look back to this torture and thank us. (Oh, and by the way, you're welcome.)

OK, for your next two exercises, we shift into reverse and try the *pull-off* versions of the last two workouts. The first one, is the four-notes-per-string version, using all four fret-hand fingers.

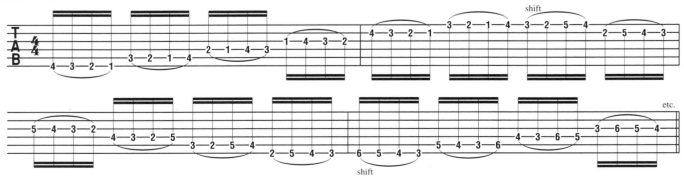

And here is the triplet pull-off version, played with your fret hand's middle, ring, and pinky fingers.

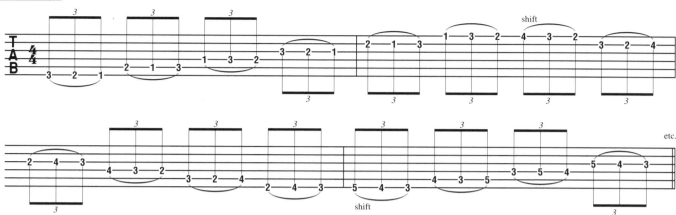

With all four of these exercises, continue the pattern all the way up to the 12th fret. Practice these every day, if possible, and always use a metronome. As you've probably figured out by now, these exercises are a *serious* workout. Take breaks when you need them, because your left hand, and especially your forearm, are gonna get pretty sore. The old adage, "no pain, no gain," does *not* apply to the muscles in your forearms and hands. If you feel pain, stop immediately and take a break.

Three-Notes-Per-String Scales

A very common application of the legato technique is to play scalar runs using patterns that comprise three notes per string. This is a good way to get all four fingers involved in the legato process.

Let's start with an ascending G major scale in triplets. Pick only once for each new string.

 What goes up, must come down, so when you reach the eighth fret on the first string, slide your pinky finger up to the tenth fret and then descend the G major scale using this finger pattern.

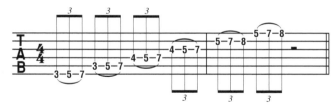 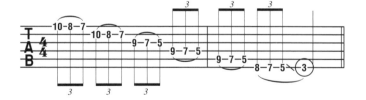

Now let's put those two together for one fluid, scalar run. Strive for a smooth sound and a consistent volume throughout.

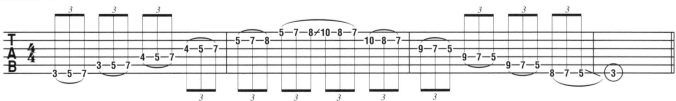

You can turn this lick into a great exercise, too, by continuing up the fretboard to every position of the G major scale. You'll essentially be playing through all seven modes of G major. These modes are indicated below the tab staff. Use a tempo slow enough that you can play through the entire exercise without stopping and while staying in rhythm.

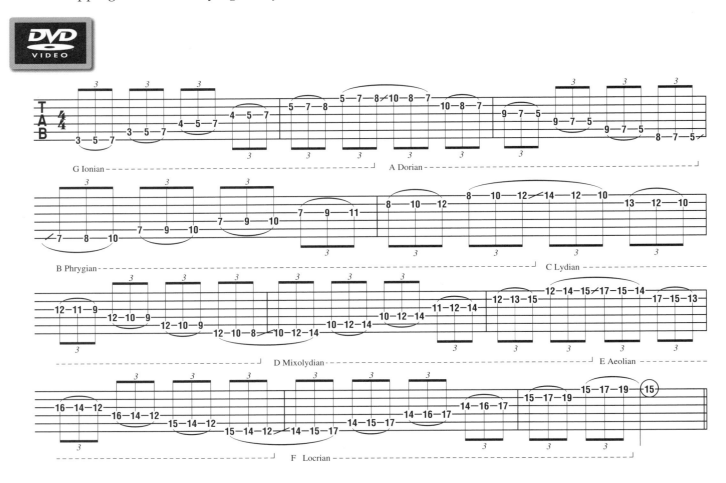

One common pitfall that players tend to fall into when using legato technique is letting the finger patterns dictate the rhythms. In other words, if they're playing three notes per string, they always play triplets or sextuplets. If they're playing a scale pattern that contains two notes per string—like the minor pentatonic—they play in eighth or sixteenth notes. It's important to be able to place the accent anywhere in the legato phrase. Mastering that discipline will free you up to use any rhythm you want.

To get you started on your quest to rhythmic freedom, let's play the G major scale you just played, only in a sixteenth-note rhythm instead of triplets. And as you play through the scale, accent each downbeat. If it's a picked note, strike it a little harder. If the downbeat occurs on a hammer-on or pull-off, use a little more force than on other notes.

Now let's try playing an A minor pentatonic scale, which has two notes per string in its pattern, but in a triplet rhythm, so that the accent appears on each downbeat. Like the last exercise, it's tough, but an essential skill worth developing.

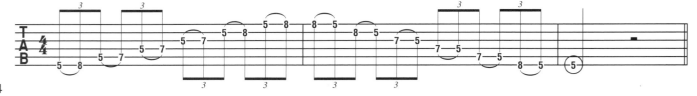

14

"Hammer-on from Nowhere"

When executing hammer-ons and pull-offs, you've so far had to provide a pick attack to initiate the move. But that's not always necessary. Many top legato players will use the *hammer-on from nowhere* technique when descending a scalar line, for improved speed and uniformity of sound.

The concept is pretty simple. When you're moving from one string *down* to a lower string, you don't need to use the pick. Instead you hammer onto the target fret with the appropriate fretting finger. It takes a fair bit of force, and it works best with a distorted sound, but it makes for an exciting weapon in your legato arsenal. Here's how it sounds with an A minor pentatonic scale.

Some adventurous players will also use this technique when ascending, but it's more difficult because you have to time the hammer-on with the release of another finger, whereas you don't have that problem when you're descending. Still, it's worth spending some time on the technique.

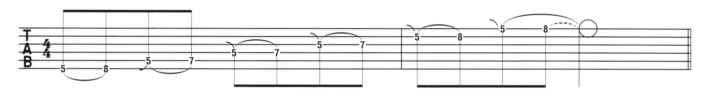

Hammer-ons from nowhere don't really come to life when used in the context of playing scales, so let's check out some licks that make use of this flashy technique.

This first one is a descending sixteenth-note lick in E minor that repeats an octave lower. It's a killer rock lick, in the style of guitarist George Lynch, but the best part is that you pick only *once*, at the beginning, and that's it.

This next lick, in A minor, adds a new challenge in that it contains many different rhythms, making it more of a "real-life" musical example. Note that in bar 2, the descent down the A minor scale is played in 32nd notes. You can approach this rhythm in two ways. The first: simply play it as fast as you can. OK, not really. The best way to approach it is to think of it as two sets of four sixteenth notes played in the space of a single beat.

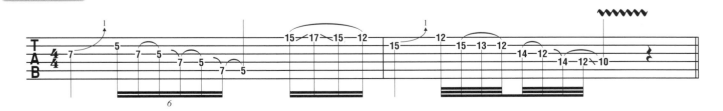

This next lick mixes A Dorian with the A blues scale. You could use this lick over a rock boogie or shuffle, like Joe Satriani's "Satch Boogie" or David Lee Roth's "Bump and Grind."

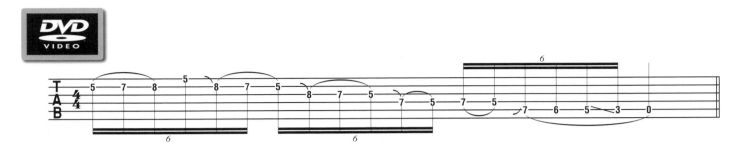

Here's one that uses well-placed shift slides to descend two full octaves in D minor. Like the previous lick, this one is arranged in a sextuplet rhythm, which means every note is evenly spaced. Use these two licks to work on achieving evenness of tempo and volume.

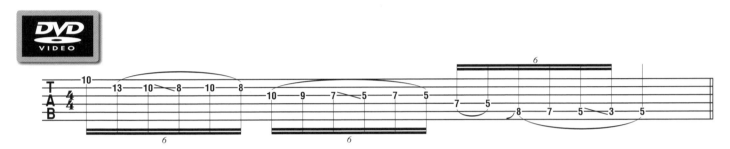

Single-String Legato Lines

Another common application of legato technique is to create single-string phrases, where you traverse the neck along one string using nothing but hammers, pull-offs, and slides. Though popular among shredders, blues rockers like Jimi Hendrix and Stevie Ray Vaughan also used this technique to great effect.

 Here's a lick that travels down the G major pentatonic scale, all along the third string.

Some players like to use this technique with sort of a rhapsodic rhythm, which can create a slithery, sinuous effect. You just basically pick a scale, pick a string, strike it once, and then let your fingers do the walking.

Here's an example with a G Mixolydian line. The rhythm is somewhat advanced; if you're having trouble, use the performance on the DVD as your guide, to get a good feel for it.

Now let's check out some famous legato runs as employed by the masters. Texas virtuoso Eric Johnson opens up one of his instrumental classics, "Zap," with a burning line from the F minor pentatonic scale. Although Johnson can pick as well as anyone, here he employs hammer-ons, pull-offs, and slides throughout to achieve a smooth, uniform sound.

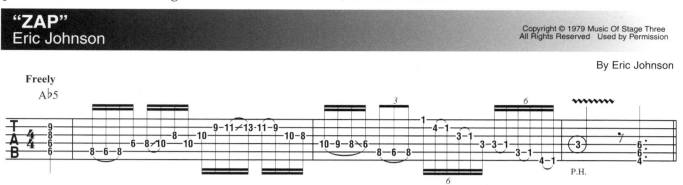

Steve Vai demonstrates why he reigns as one of the true masters of the legato technique with this climactic, descending C major scale flurry during his gut-wrenching "Tender Surrender" solo. Notice the use of the "hammer-on from nowhere" several times throughout for a truly "look ma, no right hand" effect!

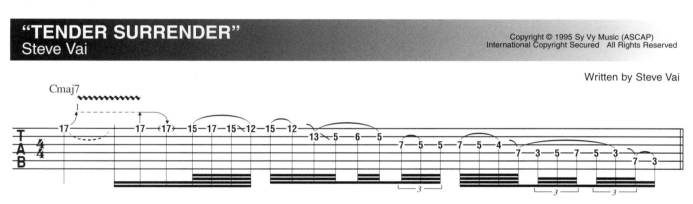

Yngwie caps off the chorus of "Rising Force" with a blazing three-notes-per-string legato descent through E harmonic minor. If triplets seem a bit slow for the Swedish shredmaster, keep in mind that the tempo is a mere 248 bpm!

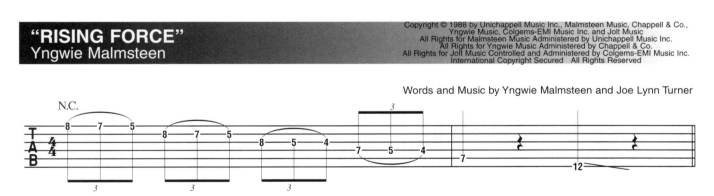

When it comes to legato playing, Eddie Van Halen is best known for his revolutionary two-handed tapping technique, but his traditional legato lines are equally amazing. One of Van Halen's favorite moves is to mix legato and pick attacks in sequenced phrases, as he does in this excerpt from his acoustic shred clinic "Spanish Fly."

Even though the time signature changes from 4/4 to 7/8 to 3/4 in the course of just three measures, the phrasing feel is triplets throughout, so focus on maintaining even temporal spacing between picked and legato sequences.

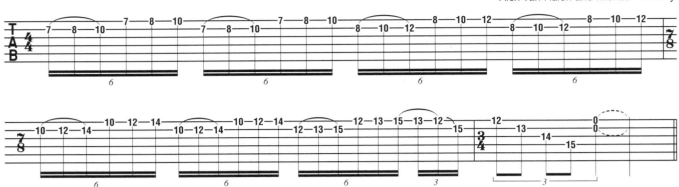

Iron Maiden's eighties metal anthem, "Aces High," is treated is to a classic open-string pull-off lick courtesy of Dave Murray. He wraps up the phrase with a speedy and slippery ascending run through an A minor scale pattern in twelfth position.

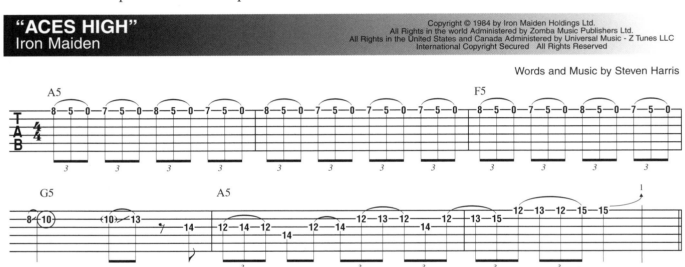

And to close out this legato lesson, we look to legato legend Allan Holdsworth. But you might want to do some serious finger stretches first. With his large hands, Holdsworth often injected large-interval jumps on the same string, and frequently employed four-notes-per-string sequences in his seamless legato phrases. Here are the final five and a half bars of his solo to "Road Games," for just a taste of his deliciously liquid lines.

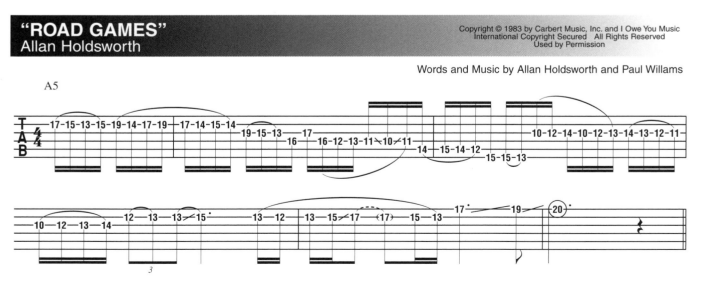

Two-Handed Tapping

In the mid-'70s, a skinny young Dutch kid named Eddie Van Halen was lighting up the L.A. rock club scene with a monster sound and a mysterious new technique—mysterious because he played with his back to the audience whenever he used it. But in 1978, when his band's self-titled debut, *Van Halen* was unleashed for all the world to hear, Van Halen's secret was out, and he was on his way to securing his place among the most influential guitarists the world has ever known.

Even though guitarists such as Steve Hackett (Genesis), Frank Zappa, and Brian May were using tapping techniques before him, and players including Reb Beach, Vito Bratta, and Jeff Watson have raised the bar since, Eddie Van Halen was, is, and will always be *the man* when it comes to two-handed tapping. And it all starts, of course, with his famous guitar solo, "Eruption," which contained a massive barrage of arpeggios played faster than any guitarist had ever heard.

Tapping Triads

Since this arpeggio application is probably the easiest tapping technique to master, it's a good place to start. The basic technique involves tapping one note and playing two notes with your fretting hand. Every note will be tapped, pulled off, or hammered on, so you don't need your pick at all—but you will have to figure out what to do with your pick while you're tapping.

Because Eddie holds his pick between his thumb and middle finger, his index finger is free to execute his tapping lines. But even Eddie shoves his pick in his mouth or in the knuckle of his middle finger, so he can better stabilize his tapping hand on the neck. If you want to emulate Eddie, you can do the same, or you can follow the lead of other tapping wizards like Reb Beach, who uses his middle finger to do all his tapping while holding his pick in place between his thumb and index finger. There is no "right" or "wrong" way to do it; experiment with each of the approaches and use the one that's best for you.

Now, let's take a look at a tapped A minor arpeggio, all on the first string. As you play the example, be sure to mute the lower strings with the palm of your tapping hand so they don't start ringing out.

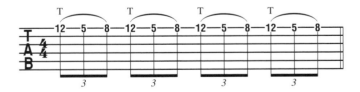

This is the intervallic arrangement heard in "Eruption," and thus the most commonly used one. But there are all sorts of variations you can use to create new licks. For starters, you can simply reverse the order of the notes on the fifth and eighth frets, like this.

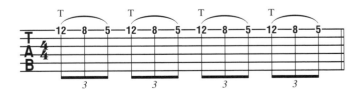

Or you can alternate their order mid-lick, like this.

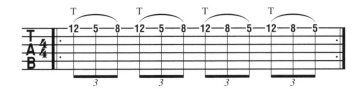

Those are two of the more common variations, but for real adventure, try placing notes other than the tapped one on the downbeat. To sound the first note, just do a silent pull-off with your tapping finger. You're basically just plucking the string on the neck instead of down by the bridge and pickups as you would do with a normal pick attack.

Here are four variations using this concept.

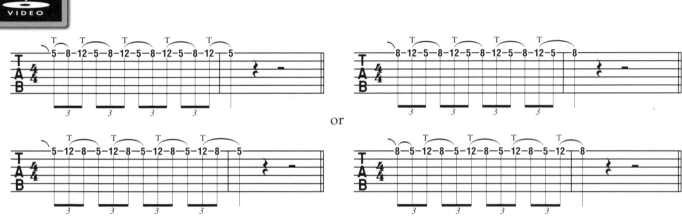

or

Obviously, you're not going to go through life tapping on just the high E string. You can take this same three-note concept and move it to different strings to create various arpeggios. As you move from string to string, muting may become an issue, but it's an easy one to handle. As a rule, you'll use your tapping hand's palm to mute all of the strings lower than the one you're using, and the underside of your fret hand's index finger to mute the strings higher than the one you're using. Use this approach on the following example.

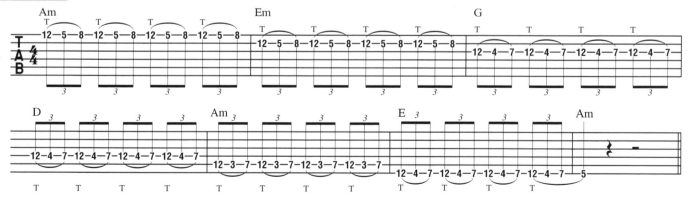

Another approach commonly used in tapping sequences is to play different arpeggios up and down a single string. This next example takes you through a G–Am–Bm–C–D–G progression, all via tapping on the first string. The challenge here is to make the position shifts without losing a beat. As always, use a metronome and set it at a speed that allows you to play the passage without losing the groove or making a mistake.

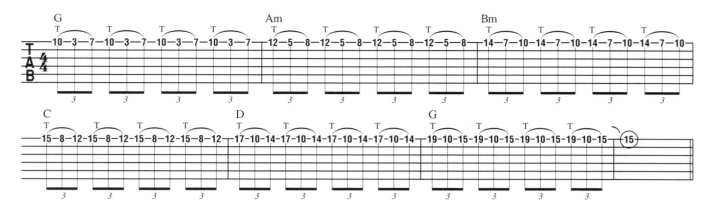

Now, if you got through that one OK, you're ready to give the tapping section of "Eruption" a go. Here are the first eight bars of Van Halen's tapping bonanza.

"ERUPTION"
Van Halen

Music by David Lee Roth, Edward Van Halen,
Alex Van Halen and Michael Anthony

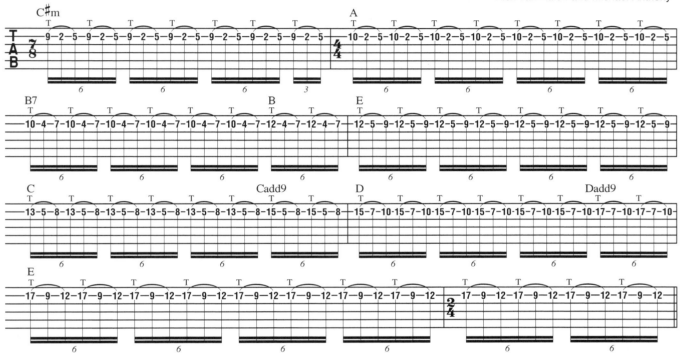

Since you're dealing with a three-note triad shape, triplet rhythms are obviously very common. But you can turn them into 16th-note licks just by doubling up on one of the fret-hand notes. The first pattern is a step-wise walk down and back up an A minor arpeggio.

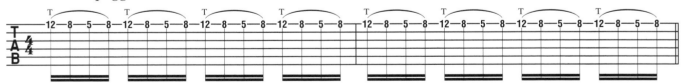

This second sixteenth-note tapping pattern turns the root, A, fretted with your index finger, into a pedal tone.

Scalar Fragments

The tapping technique is certainly not limited to use with arpeggios. Simply adding a diatonic scale tone to your fret hand's duties creates a *scalar fragment*, which you can then use to play sizzling sixteenth-note tapping lines, like this descending phrase from the A minor scale.

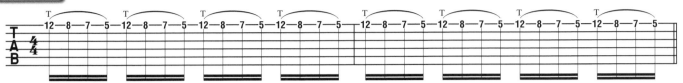

Adding just that one extra note also greatly expands the phrasing variations available to you. Here are just a few of possibilities using this four-note pattern, each starting with the tapped note.

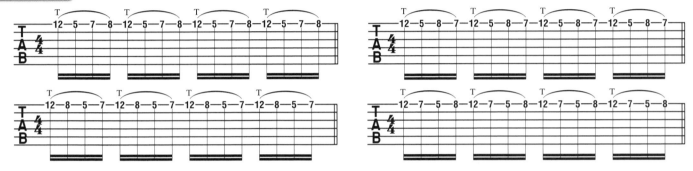

Just like you did with the three-note arpeggio patterns earlier, you can start these four-note scalar fragments on a note other than the tapped one, using a "silent pull-off" executed with your tapping finger. Here are four variations using this approach.

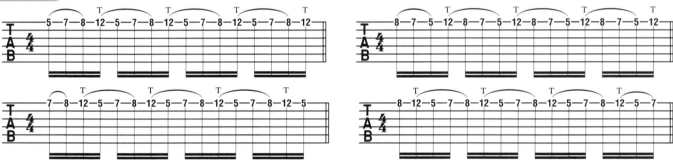

Now let's take a look at some tapping licks using these variations. This first one is a fiery, descending line in G.

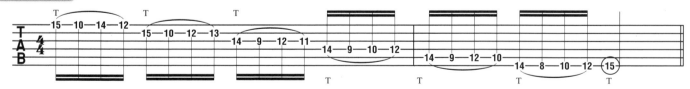

And here's one that ascends the D minor scale along the second string. While you're tapping finger is doing its job, shift your fret hand up to the next position.

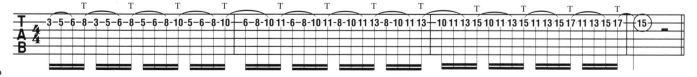

Ascending Tapping Licks and Patterns

So far, we've only played with licks and exercises that either descend across the strings or move horizontally along just one string. But you can also tap your way *up* through the strings. Because of the physical layout of the guitar, and the fact that few guitarists spend any time performing hammer-ons with their fret-hand index finger, ascending phrases are more difficult than descending ones, but with practice, this skill will set you apart from the crowd.

To begin, let's ascend two octaves of a G major scale using this approach.

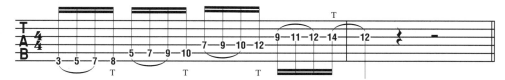

When using the tapping technique to ascend scales or licks, you have two options for moving to the next higher string. You can either hammer onto the string with your fret hand's index finger, or you can use a right-hand finger to pluck the string directly after you tap.

Tapping master Reb Beach, of Winger fame, uses the latter technique, as he says that it provides the most seamless, fluid sound. Judging by the tapping phrases in his solos to such Winger hits as "Seventeen" and "Headed for a Heartbreak," he's right. Try both ways and see what feels best for you. Then give that G major scale another whack, but this time take it up a full three octaves, across all six strings.

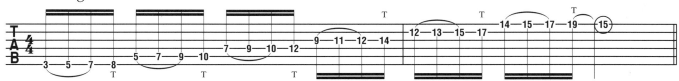

Learning and mastering ascending tapping technique opens up a whole new realm of possibilities, including ascending pentatonic licks and arpeggios. Let's try a few, shall we? Here's a great E minor pentatonic ascending tapping lick, to get you started.

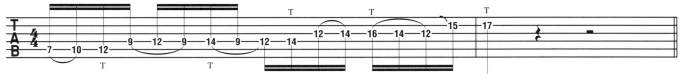

Here's another E minor pentatonic tapping lick, but this one includes ascending and descending contours on each string, and incorporates a variation used by Eddie Van Halen in "Hot For Teacher" and Joe Satriani in "Satch Boogie"—the use of open strings.

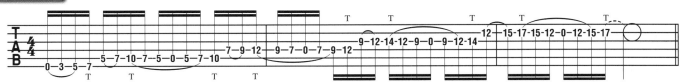

You can also use ascending tapping patterns to fabricate multi-octave arpeggios, a technique used by guitarist Nuno Bettencourt in Extreme's "Get the Funk Out." Because of the large interval leaps achieved with the tapping approach, you'll typically need to skip strings when tapping multi-octave arpeggios. This will make the plucking method of sounding the first note on the next higher string a little more difficult, and it makes the hammer-on method slightly easier. Still, try it both ways to see which approach works best for you.

Here's an A major arpeggio that ascends and descends on strings 5, 3, and 1.

Tapped Bends

By now you've come to see there are nearly endless possibilities for unique and dazzling phrasing when using the tapping technique. But believe it or not, we've only just begun.

One of the most effective techniques used by rock guitarists to create expressive phrasing string-bending. Well, who says you can't bend strings and tap at the same time? Truth is, you can, and the combination can sound downright sublime.

To begin, bend a note with your fret hand, as you normally would, and then tap onto a higher fret while the note is still bent. You can then let it ring, or pull off to the fretted bent note. Here's an example.

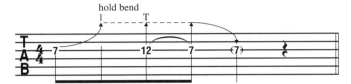

When you consider pre-bends, bend-and-releases, and the various orders of notes, you'll find tons of variations possible for this type of lick. Here are just a few.

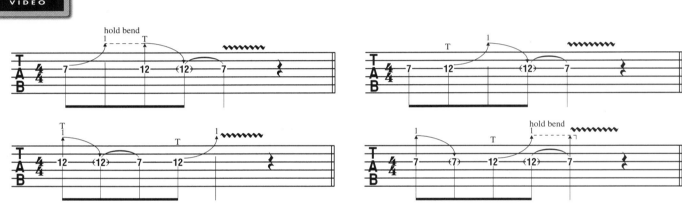

You can also play "normal" licks with this technique to give them a totally different sound. For example, here's a basic A minor pentatonic lick, fretted in the traditional manner.

Now, compare that with this version, using tapped bends. By the way, to produce vibrato on a tapped note, use your fretting hand to shake the string as you normally would, letting your tapping finger stay on for the ride.

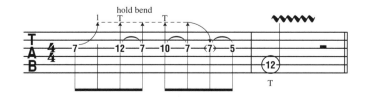

Tapped Slides

Besides bending tapped notes, you can also *slide* them. Here's an E minor pentatonic sequence on the B string, using tapped slides.

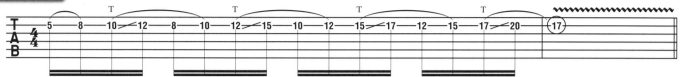

For most guitarists, moving a tapping finger up and down a string is a whole new skill that will take some time to develop the "muscle memory" to make the technique seamless. So the key here, as usual, is to play at a tempo slow enough that you can execute the techniques cleanly and in time, while developing said "muscle memory."

Here's a descending lick from the E blues scale, for a different angle on the technique.

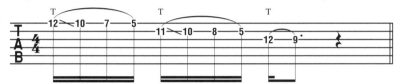

And, of course, you can combine tapped bends and tapped slides into one lick for a completely novel sound. Here's a B minor pentatonic lick that does just that.

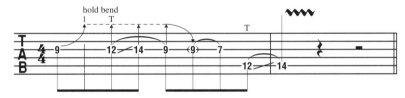

OK, now let's take a look at some famous tapping sequences that employ the concepts taught in this lesson. The first example contains the first seven and a half bars of Van Halen's "Hot for Teacher," into which Eddie Van Halen incorporates position shifts along a single string, pull-offs to open strings, and movement across strings.

Words and Music by David Lee Roth, Edward Van Halen, Alex Van Halen and Michael Anthony

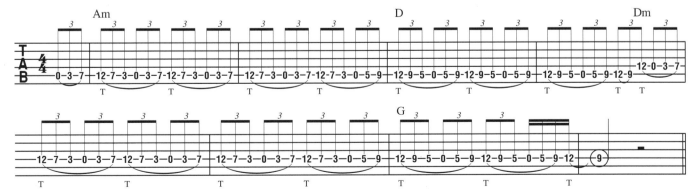

As we mentioned earlier, achieving fluid and seamless *ascending* legato lines is a challenging task, but it's one that Winger guitarist Reb Beach has made look easy throughout his career. A proponent of the tap-and-pluck approach, Beach has said his goal was to make his ascending tapping runs sound smooth as a saxophone, and this E minor tapping lick from his solo in "Seventeen" certainly meets that criterion. Note Beach's tasty tap-and-slide technique, too.

"SEVENTEEN"
Winger

Words and Music by Kip Winger, Reb Beach and Beau Hill

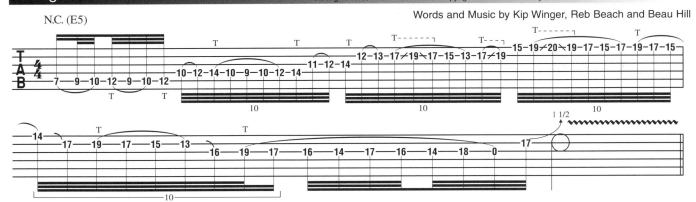

In pop culture circles, guitarist Nuno Bettencourt is best known for his pluck 'n' slap acoustic fretwork in Extreme's 1990 crossover smash "More Than Words." But among guitar players, Bettencourt is revered more for his monster chops than his monster ballads—a reputation well-earned as made evident by the tapped arpeggios in his solo on "Get the Funk Out." The following four bars of fretboard acrobatics are tough, but you may find them easier than it appears. Take your time to make the line sound as fluid as possible, particularly on the string skips and position shifts, and then concentrate on the rhythm.

"GET THE FUNK OUT"
Extreme

Words and Music by Nuno Bettencourt and Gary Cherone

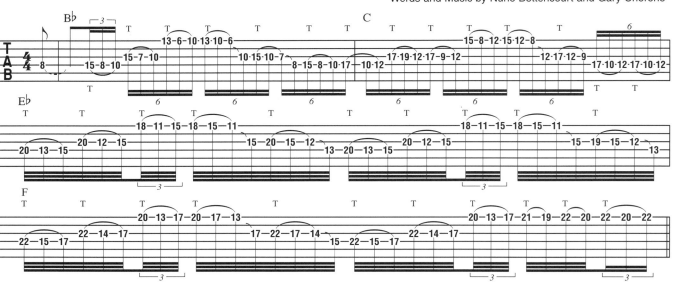

In 1987, White Lion hit the hair metal circuit with "Wait," a smash hit buoyed by guitarist Vito Bratta's tasty tapfest in the song's solo. Truly a composition within a composition, Bratta combined tapped bends, tapped slides, legato slides, and tapped arpeggios to create one of the most expressive guitar solos not just of the hair metal era, but of all time. Here are the opening five and a half bars.

"WAIT"
White Lion

Words and Music by Mike Tramp and Vito Bratta

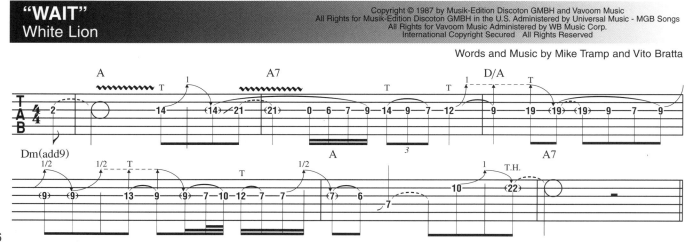

Sweep Picking

Just as Eddie Van Halen turned the guitar world upside down with his revolutionary tapping technique a few years earlier, when Yngwie Malmsteen hit American shores in 1983 with his debut, *Rising Force*, guitarists were once again sent back to the woodshed to work not only on their alternate picking chops but also on a new technique: sweep picking. A most economical approach to playing arpeggios, proper sweep picking can vastly improve the efficiency and speed of your picking hand.

The rationale for sweep picking is simple: when playing a phrase that contains only one note per string, like an arpeggio, it's faster to use consecutive strokes in the same direction when moving from string to string, rather than alternating ones. While shredders like Malmsteen, Jason Becker, and Tony MacAlpine exploited the sweep picking technique masterfully on arpeggios, others, like Frank Gambale, used it *any* time they switched strings.

Seduced by the speed attainable through sweep picking, too many guitarists try to jump right in and start sweeping at full tempo. You can't make a bigger mistake. In this lesson, we're going to break down the technique to its essential elements and show you the correct sweeping technique, so you'll be sweeping through arpeggios and licks in no time.

Proper Pick-Hand Technique

Sweep picking is a simple concept but it requires a lot of refinement and practice. All swept notes should sound as clear, separate, and rhythmically accurate as cleanly alternate-picked notes sound. Both the pick hand and fret hand will contribute to its clean execution.

The first step on your road to mastering sweep picking is to isolate the picking hand's part of the technique. To do so, here's an example that uses the top three open strings, so you don't have to think at all about the fretting hand for now.

Start with a downstroke on the third string, but rather than moving your pick away from the guitar as you would with a normal downstroke, follow through straight down and rest your pick against the next string. Next, pick the second string and let the pick follow through and come to rest against the first string. Finally, pick the first string. When sped up, the consecutively grouped downstrokes are actually executed in one continuous motion called a *downsweep*.

As you perform the downsweep, make sure your wrist does not rotate, and keep the pick at the same angle, regardless of which string you're playing or in which direction you're moving. The sweeping movement comes from extending (downsweeps) and flexing (upsweeps) the entire arm. Focus on pushing the pick through each string as it moves toward the next one, and don't let the string resistance change the posture of your hand. That way the pick is still in the proper position when it's time to start an upsweep.

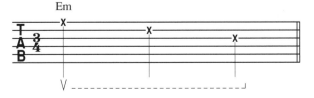

Now let's change direction and perform the *upsweep*. Because you're working against gravity as well as the string's resistance, upsweeps are a little more difficult, but focus on the details of the technique, and you'll be fine. To begin, pick the first string with an upstroke, and let the pick move straight up to the bottom side of the second string. Repeat with an upstroke on the second string, coming to rest on the third, and then play an upstroke on the third string, and you've completed the upsweep.

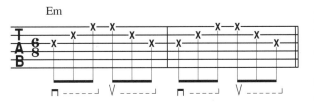

OK, let's put the two motions together now.

27

Fret-Hand Technique

When sweep picking, your fretting hand must make sure that only one tone at a time is produced, by releasing and damping the previous note, and fretting the next one only when it should sound. This is a tricky technique with a lot of subtle timing, but if you start slowly and have patience, it will come around.

To practice this move, let's apply it to a B♭maj7–Dm7 sweeping lick, in fifth position, on the top four strings. First, align your four fret-hand fingers over the frets, but don't press them down yet. Beginning with the pinky finger on the fourth string, press each finger down at the time that note is supposed to be heard, and gently release it as the next note is played. For the upsweep on the Dm7 portion, use the same process, only in reverse order.

Remember to use a metronome when practicing your sweep-picking technique. Too many guitarists, when sweep picking, cleanly play the lowest and highest notes of the phrase, with a slightly muted "scratch" comprising all the notes in the middle. Using the metronome helps to reinforce that each note of the arpeggio is equally important and thus should be equally heard.

Here's another sweep-picking exercise with which you can practice fret-hand muting. Continue the pattern up to fourteenth position, and then work back down the fretboard.

PICK-HAND MUTING

Sweep picking is usually performed while using high-gain amp settings. As a result, extraneous noise can be a real issue. To help keep your phrases clearly articulated, you'll want to use a little pick-hand palm muting. This is relatively easy to accomplish: simply let the side of your pick hand's palm brush against the strings as you pick them. With the high-gain settings typically used in the shred realm, those slightly muted notes will still jump through the speakers.

A lot of commonly used arpeggio shapes contain two or more consecutive notes played at the same fret on adjacent strings. When that happens, it's often necessary to use the same fret-hand finger, carefully rolling the tip off of one string so that the pad plays only the next one (ascending), without letting the notes ring together. And when the movement is reversed–descending from a higher to a lower string on the same fret–you have to plan ahead, playing the higher note with the finger pad so that you can then roll your finger off of that note and catch the lower one with your fingertip.

Here is an A major arpeggio that contains consecutive notes on the top two strings, at the fifth fret. Before you try that, however, practice the move on this basic two-string A5 arpeggio.

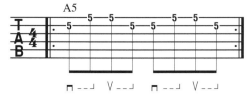
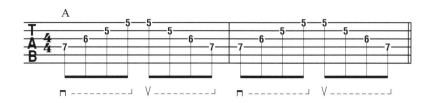

28

Next, let's extend that finger-rolling technique to three strings, using this popular A minor arpeggio shape.

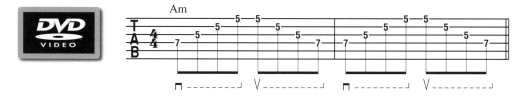

The two arpeggio shapes you just played, A major and A minor, are two of the more popular shapes used in conjunction with the sweep-picking technique. Here is a diatonic exercise in the key of G major that relies on these two shapes exclusively.

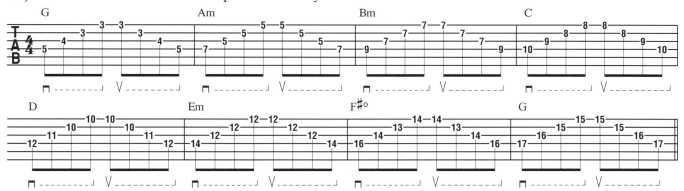

After you've played through this exercise in G, move it around to other keys as well.

Three-String Arpeggio Shapes

In addition to the four-note triad shapes you just played, sweep-picking shredders just love to use three-string triad shapes, played on the top three strings of the guitar. Here are those shapes, arranged into a sweep-picking exercise in the key of D.

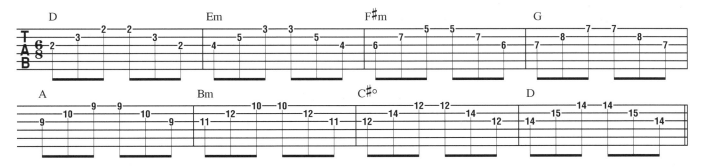

Next, we're going to toss you a curveball and add a second chord tone to the first string of the arpeggios you just played, resulting in a seven-note sequence with alternate picking on the top string.

Here's the same D major arpeggio exercise from before, with the extra note on the first string. Use the picking directions below the first two beats for the entire exercise.

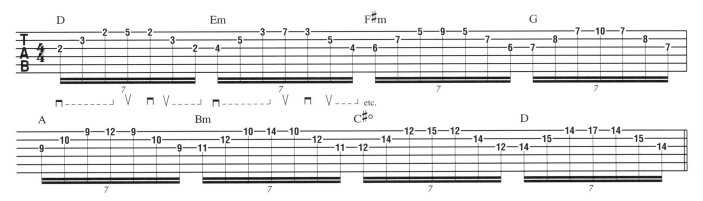

Legato + Sweep = Economy!

As you likely discovered in that last exercise, the normally efficient sweep picking pattern becomes a bit muddled when a string contains two notes. To counter this problem, most players incorporate legato technique within their sweeping licks any time more than one note appears on a given string. This allows the basic sweeping direction of the lick to go uninterrupted.

Let's take a look at that diatonic D major arpeggio exercise again, this time using a pull-off on the first string, to maintain the upsweep. Use the picking directions beneath the first two beats for the entire exercise. Your pick hand will have to pause, in rhythm, for the pull-off note to sound, before continuing with the upsweep on the second string.

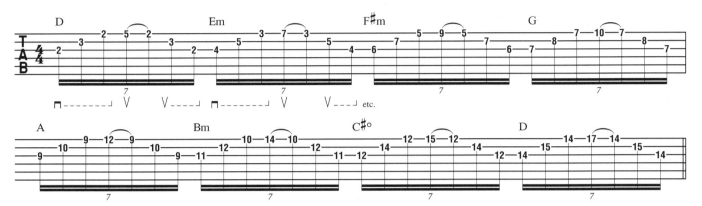

Some popular arpeggio shapes contain two notes on the lowest string of the pattern, for which you can use a hammer-on when ascending the arpeggio, and a pull-off on the descent. Each arpeggio in this next exercise, which uses the sweeping and legato techniques with diatonic triad arpeggios in the key of B minor, contains two notes on the fifth string.

Remember, your picking hand has to pause after the initial downstroke, while your fret hand executes the hammer-on. Also, your first, second, and third fret-hand fingers use the rolling technique in both directions at some point in the exercise. These contribute to the exercise's considerable level of difficulty, but they're part of the whole sweeping deal.

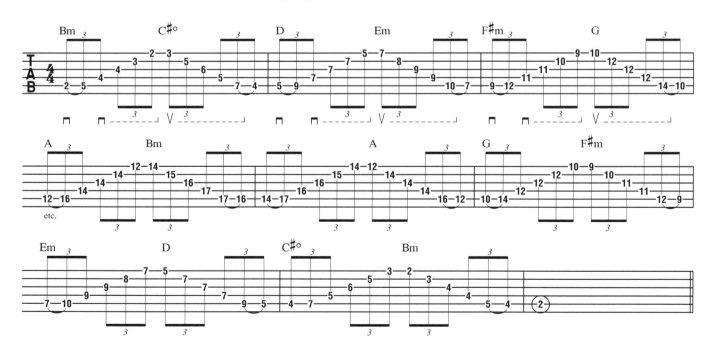

As tempting as it might be, don't rush the sweeps or let your hands get out of sync. If you really want to learn how to sweep pick properly, you've got to practice with a metronome, keeping the exercises clean and accurate as you gradually build speed. After a few months, the results will be downright awesome.

On these final two pages, we'll take a look at some sweep-picking licks as used by the shred masters.

This first sweep-picking lick comes courtesy of the king of modern shred guitar, Yngwie Malmsteen, and his breakthrough instrumental, "Black Star." When the solo changes key from E minor to A minor, Malmsteen lets rip with this two-octave A minor arpeggio.

"BLACK STAR"
Yngwie Malmsteen

By Yngwie Malmsteen

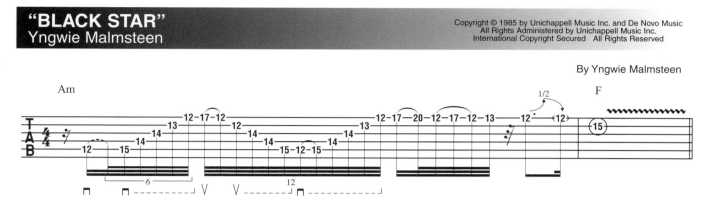

Another classic Malmsteen sweep-picking move is the ascending diminished seventh arpeggio, as heard in the intro to "Far Beyond the Sun."

"FAR BEYOND THE SUN"
Yngwie Malmsteen

By Yngwie Malmsteen

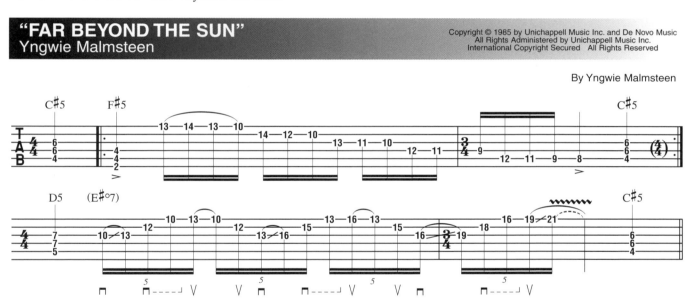

Though he doesn't use the technique often, guitarist Steve Vai on occasion will sweep through arpeggios, more for a twist on his already twisted phrasing than for harmonic reinforcement. For example, in his ballad "Blue Powder," from the revolutionary instrumental album *Passion and Warfare*, he punctuates a whammy-manipulated oblique bend in A minor with an Am arpeggio followed by Gmaj7, and then ends the phrase with a high-octane descent down the A minor pentatonic scale.

"BLUE POWDER"
Steve Vai

By Steve Vai

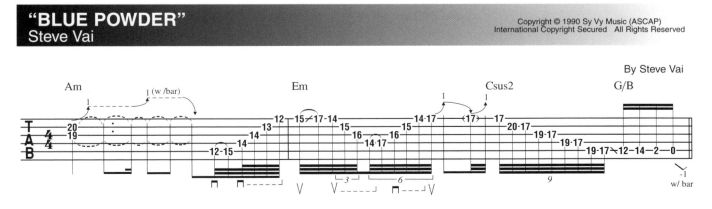

When he first hit the shred scene with Cacophony, in the mid-'80s, guitarist Marty Friedman set himself apart from other fret-burners with his affinity for exotic scales and sounds. And when he joined Megadeth, that individuality found a much bigger audience. In "Hangar 18," from Megadeth's *Rust in Peace*, Friedman tosses this sweep-picking gem into his first solo. The big lesson to take away here is Friedman's steady sixteenth-note rhythm, which contributes to the lick's fluid sound.

"HANGAR 18"
Megadeth

Words and Music by Dave Mustaine

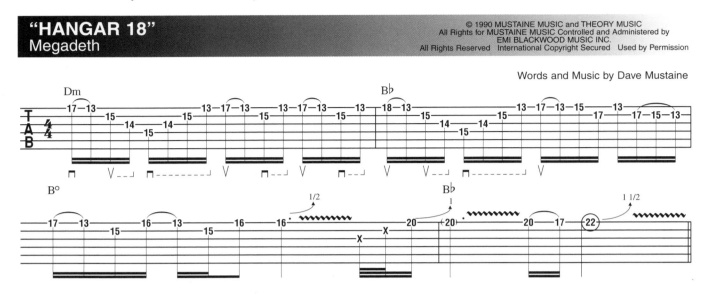

Our final sweep-picking example comes from the world of classical music. Composer and violinist Niccolo Paganini was in many ways the world's first "rock star." He had long, flowing hair, a flamboyant stage style, and a controversial lifestyle—including rumors of Satanic collusion. And when you consider the virtuosic nature of his pieces, you could call Paganini the first "shredder," as well.

The 24th Caprice is likely Paganini's most famous composition, written in a theme and variation form. The first variation, arranged here for guitar as played by shredder Michael Fath, is essentially a sweep-picking exercise. There are a few awkward position shifts necessary to pull this off, so focus not only on a steady rhythm within the sweep-picked arpeggios but also on maintaining the pulse between them.

"CAPRICE NO. 24"
Niccolo Paganini

By Niccolo Paganini

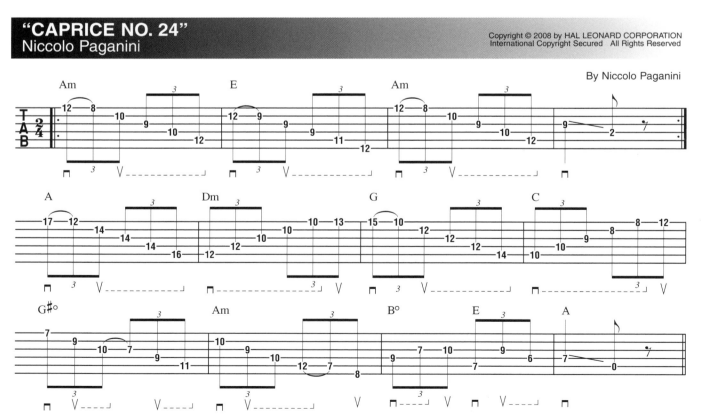

Landscape Conserv

Landscape Conservation

By

Brian Hackett

Emeritus Professor of Landscape Architecture
University of Newcastle-upon-Tyne

PACKARD PUBLISHING LTD.
Chichester

Produced and designed in association with
Book Production Consultants, 7 Brooklands Avenue,
Cambridge CB2 2BB.

Printed and bound in the United Kingdom by
The Burlington Press (Cambridge) Ltd., Foxton, Cambridge CB2 6SW.

Contents

Introduction

Landscape all over the world is undergoing change — in the countryside it is affected by new agricultural and forestry techniques, mineral extraction and factory industries, while the urban landscape is also changing as a result of concentrations of population and activities as well as other influences such as atmospheric pollution. A narrow-minded nation allows these changes to take place regardless of action to conserve some of the fine wild and humanized landscapes and to introduce measures for the safeguarding of newly shaped landscapes of quality — when conservation and safeguarding cannot fail to benefit ourselves and our descendants.

There is, however, a growing interest in conserving landscape, sometimes as a strict preservation process and sometimes in an acceptable modified form to meet the current economic and social changes. Also, there is a growing realization that newly shaped landscapes need surveillance if they are to retain their character. New laws and directives have resulted from this interest, and any list of them requires additions almost as soon as it is printed.

It is difficult to write about landscape conservation without considering rural and urban planning matters, but I have tried to avoid too much discussion on these, despite their importance, in the hope that all who make changes to the environment will remember that landscape is the basis of environment. Economic and social changes affecting the landscape often take little account of the fact that landscape has all those qualities associated with life, and that change needs to be tempered with respect for these qualities. Thus, landscape conservation cannot be likened to an organism preserved in a bottle in a museum, but needs the idea of renewal, whether as an exact replacement or merely retaining the original concept.

Many skills are involved in operations concerned with rural and urban landscape, and landscape conservation works draw upon these skills. The Bibliography will direct the reader to sources of information on these skills. My thanks to all those persons who have given permission to quote from their writings and who have made available many of the illustrations.

Brian Hackett
Jesmond 1980.

Chapter 1

Landscapes for conservation

The landscape is the world in which we live. Should it always be made to change as our way of life changes? Should we safeguard its inherent fertility, but allow its appearance to change with new agricultural and forestry techniques? Or should we have a plan which keeps the best, the most interesting, and the most representative of past cultural achievements, whilst allowing controlled change to take place in other areas? The present interest in the environment, plus genuine fears that technical advancement is outstepping the assessment of its impact, points to a firm 'yes' to the last question, and this means the conservation of landscapes developed in historic times as well as conserving the inherent fertility and special beauty of landscapes which may be changed in our own times. Conservation, as defined in the Conservation and Land Drainage Guidelines of the Water Space Amenity Commission[1] – 'the harmonisation of man's activities with the natural environment' – also means controlling change in other than 'wild' and natural landscapes in a way which accords with this definition; and the lead should be given in Britain by Ministers of the Crown and public bodies who are charged with this duty under Act of Parliament.[2]

Preserving an historic work of art or a building requires a particular range of techniques, as well as thereafter controlling temperature and humidity, or protecting from the weather and atmospheric pollution. But landscape is different, having those characteristics associated with life – growth, death and regeneration – and comprising both moving and static living organisms, such as animals and vegetation, although the transportation of seeds gives movement to vegetation. Even the inorganic components of landscape, like the rocks and the climate, unite to become soil, albeit a slow process of change. Because of these characteristics of life and death, the history of man and other living creatures with small life spans can only be preserved in books and various illustrative media, or temporarily in folk museums and theatrical performances. Preserving historic landscape is more realistic because the inorganic components and the living organisms are slow to change in substance and appearance.

Historic landscapes can still be enjoyed for themselves and for their representation of our cultural heritage, and indeed sometimes earn their keep; for these reasons, many people wish to see them conserved. They cannot be preserved entirely in their true original form because the vegetation is now of another generation, and the water in the soil, and in lakes and streams, will have been replaced many times; it is fortunate that landscapes are able to continue to exist through renewal unless interfered with or in some other form if reverting to the natural state. Those landscapes keeping the form in which they were shaped and planted at a particular time in the past can

Overleaf

1.1 *The Timberden Valley at Shepherds Barn in Kent is an example of an Area of Outstanding Natural Beauty which has figured in a public inquiry into the proposed M25 Sevenoaks to Swanley link road. Although the landscape of many of the statutory AONBs is the result of agricultural and forestry operations, the onlooker often is not conscious of this fact, and regards them as the work of nature. The beauty of the Timberden Valley well justifies that it should be protected and that proposed changes to areas of AONB status should be subject to the Public inquiry procedure. (Courtesy of Ianthe Ruthven)*

justifiably be called historic landscapes, and many of them still have a useful role in the modern world. We can say the same about landscapes of quality which have been developed in our own times and may eventually become historic landscapes.

The safeguarding of landscape is often a major issue in public inquiries about development proposals which will change the landscape's character, and frequently arguments in its defence range around one or more of the historic, aesthetic and ecological aspects. Of these three, aesthetic issues are difficult to present in a form acceptable to all parties, ecological effects are more easily stated and supported by scientific evidence, while historic considerations suffer from opposing evidence that change is inevitable. If a case is to be presented for retaining an historic landscape, we need to be clear about its significance and what evidence can be produced in its support.

The interested parties who appear at a public inquiry when landscape conservation issues are involved because of some development planning application are the landowner, who may be an objector if compulsory purchase is involved, external interests including people resident in nearby areas and amenity societies with, perhaps, the planning authority, and the applicant who may, in fact, be the landowner. Like the landowner, the second group may support the application with some proposals such as the reclamation of derelict land; but if the proposal apparently creates havoc in the short term in order that, in the long term, the landscape be given a new lease of life, the dilemma arises whether to support or oppose the application because support will be judged by many to act against the short term conservation interests.

1.2 *Raby Castle in Co. Durham is a building which justifies conservation. Its setting in a landscape of parkland and lakes adds considerably to its appearance, and is an example of the pronouncement made at the International Council on Monuments and Sites at Venice in 1964 to the effect that the setting of a work of architectural significance should be recognized as an historic landscape with formal recognition for conservation.*

Pronouncements of international and national standing have been made from time to time about landscapes for which a good case can be made for keeping their appearance. UNESCO at the 12th session of its General Conference, held in 1962 in Paris, adopted the *Recommendation concerning the safeguarding of the beauty and character of landscapes and sites* in which 'the safeguarding of the beauty and character of landscapes and sites is taken to mean the preservation and, where possible, the restoration of the aspect of natural, rural and urban landscapes and sites, whether natural or man-made, which have a cultural or aesthetic interest or form typical natural surroundings . . . also to supplement measures for the protection of nature'. At the 15th session in 1968, UNESCO adopted the *Recommendation concerning the preservation of cultural property endangered by public or private works*; 'cultural properties' were defined in some detail and included archaeological and historic or scientific sites, but of importance to landscape conservation was the remark

that 'cultural property also includes the setting of such property'. At the 17th session in 1972, 'cultural heritage' and 'natural heritage' were defined,[3] including in the former topographical areas and the combined works of man and of nature, and in the latter natural features. In both 'heritages', beauty or the aesthetic point of view were essential requirements.

Pronouncements more directly concerned with historic landscapes designed and/or developed by some person were made at the International Council on Monuments and Sites at Venice in 1964: both the setting for a work of architectural significance and a

1.3 *The rice fields at Iwaido in the Nara Prefecture of Japan represent a landscape developed in the past by manual labour, now being superseded by mechanical methods of cultivation. But such examples are important elements in the history of a nation's culture and some of them should be conserved, and this means continuance of the old cultivation methods which often cannot be justified on purely economic grounds. Clearly, some of these historic landscapes, whose basis was productive rather than aesthetic, ought to qualify for grant aid.*

landscape with evidence of a particular civilization, significant development, or historic event were recognized as historic landscapes. The British Garden History Society narrows the understanding of an historic garden or park to a landscape deliberately created as an ornamental environment and of historical interest as such.

The proliferation of terms in general use when reference is made to change in landscape, and which are used when argument takes place about its conservation, can be confusing. Do preservation, conservation, safeguarding, protection and restoration mean the same thing, because discussion ranges from tree preservation, through conservation areas, to the protection of ancient buildings? Our concern is with the most appropriate term for landscape. UNESCO has selected 'safeguarding', which can imply protection from outside interference whilst allowing the normal activities to continue within; 'conservation' is relevant to landscape because it suggests that some activity is taking place to prevent deterioration; 'preservation' and 'restoration' suggest leaving matters as they are or returning to an earlier situation which may be appropriate for the museum-type landscapes. It is important when a proposed change to landscape is being debated that the right term is used to match the reasons put forward for resisting the change.

The term 'historic landscape' is difficult to define. How far back in time is 'historic', since most landscapes are a development of a previous landscape – even bare mountains had a different past – and in the example of an 18th century informal replacement of a 17th century newly-made formal park, the former will probably retain some characteristics of its predecessor. Instead of seeking a date in history and arguing about it, the matter is better dealt with by first ensuring a representation of past cultural developments and changing fashions and tastes, whilst also arranging a geographical distribution of examples so that each region provides a comprehensive landscape vision of its past and takes steps to ensure that recent landscape developments are similarly conserved.

It is, perhaps, natural that one's first thoughts on historic landscapes should be for the ornamental and sophisticated, but landscapes developed for economic purposes, like agriculture and forestry, can be just as historically significant as those with only a visual or recreational purpose. J. St Bodfan Gruffydd's 'Classification of Historic Landscapes'[4] indicates the many kinds of landscape which are part of the national heritage:

I Natural Landscapes

A1.1 Limited wilderness areas.

A1.2 Natural features of antiquity, such as rare geographical or climatic (glacial) features, primeval forest and relict ecosystems.

Archaeological Landscapes

A2.1 Areas containing the remains of early man, such as dolmens, barrows, stone circles, ritualistic carved hillside figures, ridgeways, with associated landscapes.

A2.2 Hill fortifications and defensive earthworks, lynchets and early 'Celtic Fields'.

A2.3 Landscapes of Roman date associated with fortifications, roads, villas, theatres, villages.

A2.4 Vestiges of Saxon settlements and cultivation patterns, hedges, formerly forest fringe surrounding 'assorts' or property boundaries marking forest clearings, rare hedges planted to define field boundaries; wood pastures.

A2.5 Medieval strip farming still cultivated traditionally, Royal forests, early fen drainage.

A2.6 Examples of historic agricultural landscape.

A2.7 Relict designed landscapes.

Historic Landscapes forming or as part of Areas of Outstanding Natural Beauty, Conservation Areas, Areas of Great Landscape Beauty, etc.

A3.1 Rare examples of the former relationship between town and country.

A3.2 Battlefield sites.

A3.3 Historic sites.

A3.4 Industrial areas, including villages with mills, early reservoirs, spoil heaps, etc.

A3.5 Canals.

II Park and Garden Landscapes and associated Estate Landscapes planned for visual effect.

A4.1 Medieval Period – rare examples of gardens containing 'mounts' and moats, drawbridge, etc.

A4.2 16th and 17th Century – formal gardens.

A4.3 Rare vestiges of enclosure.

A4.4 18th Century – gardens and parks.

A4.5 Agricultural and village landscapes of the 18th Century.

A4.6 Estate landscapes of the 18th Century.

A4.7 Defined views (a projection of the design of a park, but beyond its physical boundaries).

A4.8 19th Century and later – formal and informal gardens.

A4.9 19th Century and later – shelter planting, coastal reclamation.

Natural landscapes, which I will define as those unaffected by man's influence since his emergence out of the wild, are often candidates for conservation because of a unique character, a special appearance or scientific interest. Generally speaking, the fewer there are of these landscapes in a country, the stronger is the case for conserving them, but several other factors are likely to affect a decision in addition to those mentioned; rarity in a national and international sense, the practical, biological and financial problems of con-

1.4 *The Roman Wall in Northumberland is one of the most familiar landscapes because of its pictorial quality as it follows the Whinsill escarpments. In order to conserve this pictorial quality, it is not just a matter of preserving the archaeological remains, which can be achieved under existing legislation, but the open pasture landscape of sheep farming needs to be safeguarded from afforestation or arable cultivation, and this is not easy to achieve. It is only necessary to imagine the Roman Wall preserved, but engulfed in a forest, to appreciate the need to conserve the whole landscape.*

serving, land ownership, the value of the land in monetary terms, and the way in which the landscape may hold back the development plans of surrounding areas are likely to tax the skill of those supporting conservation in public debate. It is not easy to ask for the conservation of natural landscapes on historical grounds because they represent the present time and not some previous state, although they are likely to be a fairly accurate representation of their appearance when the landscape had matured in the present climatic period. This gives an historic edge to the debate.

Landscapes with archaeological interest are better described as archaeological landscapes rather than historic landscapes if the archaeological interest is in artefacts, because the latter may be set in pasture land farmed in a 20th-century manner, and not regarded as historic landscape. Although not a reasoning I would consider valid, presenting landscape for conservation as archaeological rather than historic may gain more support – possibly because of the romance and excitement of archaeological discovery. When an artefact has been preserved more or less intact, a case can be made for restoring the landscape to its appearance at the time the artefact was constructed and used. But it is more likely that archaeological remains are what the words suggest, and there is no valid reason why the landscape around should be changed to the use associated with the artefact in its original state, and which does not take place today. Frequently, contemporary uses give rise to more open landscapes than prevailed in archaeological times, so the artefact may now be viewed to greater advantage. Stonehenge on Salisbury Plain gains from the open landscape around and has become a dramatic landscape feature instead of a symbol of its original obscure purpose.

A difficulty arises when the landscape around a scheduled or listed artefact of archaeological, historic, or architectural interest is not in itself of sufficient quality to be accorded conservation status, and a proposal to change the landscape is made. If this proposal would lead to a different landscape setting of equivalent quality, and thus be difficult to oppose on logical grounds, its realization may be prevented by a legal measure covering the safeguarding of the artefact or building in its setting. Even without such statutory protection of the setting, British planning authorities are required to consider the effect of any proposals in the setting upon an artefact already scheduled or listed as having special interest or merit.[5]

Under the conservation area legislation in Britain, the concept of a protected artefact is widened to cover whole areas with several buildings, groups of buildings, open spaces and trees. With both the artefact in its setting and the conservation area, there is always the problem of the endless landscape because at the boundary the protected landscape may meet a proposal for a redeveloped landscape of quite a different kind; but, of course, this is where planning authorities in Britain can act upon the 'requirement to consider', just referred to, in considering the proposal.

The emphasis on conservation centered around artefacts or buildings for a long time, and was then widened to include the setting and also landscapes designed for visual and recreational pleasure. Agricultural and afforestation landscapes with considerable visual interest have been taken for granted by most people until recent times when their historic interest and visual quality are becoming recognized. Thus, the International Symposium of Experts for the Safeguarding of Historic Landscape, held in Japan in 1977, defined an historic landscape as 'one which has had associated with it an event or a series of events of historical note. An historic landscape may also be the visual perception of a particular period of civilization, a way of life and patterns of living.'[6] The discussions at this Symposium ranged from rural and urban landscapes, to coastal regions as well as areas where traditional methods were followed in agriculture, folk crafts and industries, and other occupations. If this definition and the discussions which accompanied it are accepted as the enlightened view of historic landscape now current, examples of traditional agricultural methods and crafts, which are in danger of disappearing, will need to be safeguarded and in most cases there is a landscape associated with them.

Keeping alive traditional methods when the economic and social structure has changed so radically does mean in the majority of cases some

1.5 *The most difficult landscapes to conserve from the technical point of view are those formed as a result of an ancient method of cultivation. If conscious levelling or many years of ploughing had taken place on this example of ancient cultivation, the terracing effect would have disappeared. The solution is to continue cultivation in a way approximating to the original method. If this kind of landscape is left untouched, it would gradually be covered with a natural tree and shrub cover. Alternatively, today's farmer finds this kind of landscape expensive to cultivate unless he can use it for grazing.*

outside financial assistance and operatives and crafts-men trained in ways other than those generally practised today. It does seem surprising that a moment in history can be preserved by scheduling some artefact, with accompanying financial aid, but when the 'moment' is a living example of history in the form of landscape, although possibly on the verge of extinction, its conservation cannot be achieved through direct legislation in Britain for listing and scheduling.

The problems involved in conserving historic land-scape can be clearly stated, although support for putting conservation measures and practice into effect is often difficult to find. Conserving quality rural land-scape, which is not accepted as historic landscape, is more complicated; for example, a rural landscape may still have its hedgerows and copses, while having modern agricultural techniques applied, but the land-scape will be at risk because these techniques encourage application over large single areas and it is a temptation to root out the hedgerows to form the larger areas. The findings of the Social Science Research Council project into farmers' attitudes to conservation include the observation that there is con-siderable variety in the attitudes — the private land-owner of a large family estate may not be tied com-pletely by economic constraints on farming practice, while the small family farmer may not be able to afford the capital to embark upon major changes affecting the landscape.[7] Between these two different attitudes, which do not act contrary to conservation, the study found considerable variation in farmers' attitudes to landscape conservation.

The different types of farming have their typical landscapes, each with particular conservation problems. The upland pastures are unlikely to change much in appearance with new techniques in livestock farming, but they are subject to the temptation of ready cash and release from a hard isolated existence which is offered by afforestation agencies. The argu-ment for the conservation of upland pastures is com-plicated by the fact that historically the landscape had a sparse tree cover and was not open grassland, while visually the open pastures are generally regarded as high quality landscape; so the conservation-minded person is torn between accepting the replacement of tree cover, even if a different kind, and conserving the open pasture landscape which is likely to involve the upkeep of the dry stone walls and continuing a type of farming which does not seem attractive in the present social and economic climate.

In the lowlands, land drainage works, often encouraged by Government grants, can alter the ecology by lowering the water table, thus changing the natural vegetation and, in turn, the bird, insect and other animal populations. In extreme cases, wetlands become drylands as a result of land drainage. This dilemma is expressed in the Conservation and Land Drainage Guidelines of the Water Space Amenity Commission: 'Unfortunately such landscapes (where water-courses can be identified as being of funda-mental importance) often coincide with intensively farmed areas, including grassland, arable and mixed farm systems. These demand efficient drainage to enable the food production potential of the land to be maximised, and the conflict with landscape ideals can be critical. In such situations it is important to identify the most important features in order that they can be conserved.'[8] Land drainage works can also speed up the loss of the old water meadows where the water table was controlled by an elaborate system of weirs and drainage channels; apart from the historic interest, the water meadows benefited from a longer growing period for the grass.

In all these different aspects of conservation, the need to remember that landscape, being alive, must be protected against anything likely to bring about the kiss of death, is paramount. Landscape is imbued with great powers of survival, but if the changes made to it are fundamental ones resulting from man's dominant position in nature, like a 'permanent' lowering of the water table, it can only survive in another form. Someone or some organization making a change of this kind should take into account the conservation issues, whether historic or present, and the importance of sustaining a fertile landscape, before deciding whether and how to proceed with the work.

Endnotes

[1] WSAC, *Conservation and Land Drainage Guidelines*, (London, 1978).

[2] E.g. The Countryside Act, 1968.

[3] UNESCO, *Recommendation concerning the protection, at national level, of the cultural and natural heritage* (Paris, 1972).

[4] J. St Bodfan Gruffydd, *Protecting Historic Landscapes* (Cheltenham, 1977).

[5] Section 28, Town & Country Planning Act, 1971.

[6] Executive Committee of ISHI *Report of the International Symposium of Experts for the Safeguarding of Historic Landscape* (Tokyo, 1977).

[7] H. Newby, C. Bell, P. Saunders, D. Rose, 'Farmers' Attitudes to Conservation', in *Countryside Recreation Review*, Vol. 2 (1977) pp. 23–30.

[8] See note 1.

Chapter 2

Conservation and change

The appearance of landscape, by which I mean the way in which vegetation and water are arranged in the topography, is an expression of the use made of it; this is true of a natural landscape kept in a particular state by the participants in its ecology as well as of a humanized landscape producing food and materials necessary to man. If the appearance of a landscape is to be conserved or reconstituted in a way relating to an historical period, the original techniques and implements are essential to achieve this with complete accuracy, which means the landscape becomes a 'museum piece' in the same category as a folk museum simulating a past way of life. There is a place for some 'museum' landscapes, maintained as authentically as possible, but the very different economy and society of present times necessitates most historical landscapes having maintenance operations carried out by modern techniques and implements, such as hand scything replaced by mechanical cutting methods. All these modern techniques and implements will almost certainly give a different cast to the appearance of a landscape. The conservation or repair of a piece of old furniture can be carried out by using the techniques originally used in its construction because this will be an operation occurring only once – quite different to the regular maintenance of landscape. A craftsman carrying out repairs to old furniture as a full-time livelihood is likely, of course, to make use of modern tools where appropriate.

Historical verisimilitude in landscape has many pitfalls, not the least being the period in history which is set for its conservation or reconstruction. This is a particular dilemma in Britain because our best known landscape contribution in history – the English School

of Landscape – often featured the removal of an earlier formal garden of quality of which some remains are extant among the later work. To which period should we seek to conserve the landscape? Should we, for example, remove rare, exotic 19th-century introductions of shrubberies and specimen trees in an 18th-century landscape of grass and tree groups? With the high cost of landscape maintenance labour today, many historical landscapes can only survive if adjustments are made to the details – perennials might have to be substituted for the succession of bedding-out plants through Spring, Summer and Autumn, thereby reducing the period of floral display but maintaining the framework of the design without inhibiting the re-introduction of bedding-out plants, if desired at some future time. Faithful restoration of the planting may not be possible because a particular species of plant has become susceptible to a pest or disease due to circumstances beyond the control of those who maintain the landscape.

In view of these difficulties, one is forced to the conclusion that historical verisimilitude can only be achieved by the fortunate few, and in most cases today this means by the Central Government or a

Overleaf

2.1 *The restored parterre garden at Hampton Court, near London. Unless detailed records exist in pictorial and written form, or sufficient remains of the original layout still exist, gardens laid out many years ago are likely, when restored, to be in the style current at the time rather than an exact copy of the original. Some differences from the layout and form of a garden from a previous age are acceptable in a restoration project because it is likely that the plants and even details of the layout would have been changed from time to time in the age in question.*

charitable trust with favourable tax exemptions, unless the landscape and attractions developed in it can attract a considerable revenue from visitors. Williamsburg in the USA and some parts of the gardens at Hampton Court in Britain are examples of very accurate historical reconstruction made possible by grants from external sources and by the money brought in by visitors. As an absolute minimum, every nation ought to have at least one museum landscape of each phase of its landscape history, but obviously, a nation's history expressed in landscape within a reasonable distance of everyone is preferable.

A policy supporting museum landscapes could lead to isolated examples of the various parts of historic landscapes – i.e. herb gardens, formal pools, or woodland groves with no common setting – instead of the examples being conceived as elements of a desig-

ned landscape; this could happen because the landscape setting to which they belonged was excluded from the conservation policy, or maintenance costs may have placed a limit on the area under the policy, and it is always possible that the owners fail to see that the whole landscape is more important than its several parts. The idea of separate elements from

2.2   *One of the best known English landscape designers in the past was Lancelot Brown, who was frequently accused of destroying formal landscape layouts of the 17th and early 18th centuries when he carried out new informal layouts associated with the English School of Landscape. Thus, faced with one historical style superimposed upon another, the dilemma is to decide which should be the basis for reconstruction. This illustration shows the remains of a formal layout at Middleton Gardens, near Charleston, South Carolina, USA, but the detail of the original design is now replaced with a carpet of grass.*

different dates and styles works satisfactorily in a conventional museum because the building is sufficiently dominant to accommodate the many historical pieces from different periods and traditions without too much discordance to the appearance. With landscape, one cannot always expect to find the same feeling of dominance that a building can give when inside.

As well as comparing the safeguarding of historic landscape with the display in conventional museum buildings, the conservation area control in Britain over an area's buildings is less rigid than when a single building has been given top grade listing, and this kind of control over an area is an example worthy of study for conserving landscape.

Historical accuracy in conservation does not always produce in landscape the best result from everybody's point of view. As an example, the builders of a 500-year-old church would not have envisaged a high density of upright gravestones in the churchyard, but this would have been the situation by the end of the 19th century after perhaps two hundred years of the

monumental mason's craft. Today, the church would be seen as the builders saw it if the gravestones were removed, and many people would appreciate the grass lawns thus formed under the trees if they were opened up as a quiet open space, yet there would be complaints that the conservation policy is not the right one because the gravestones were no longer in position. By keeping the footpaths and the trees, the main features of the landscape are retained, but an elaborate new design with stone paving, terraces, sunk gardens and stone seats is unlikely to have any historical basis with the example. Some successful

2.3 *One of the gardens at Williamsburg, USA, which has been reconstructed through very detailed historical research and generous external funds. The tree – the oriental paper mulberry – was brought to Williamsburg in the 18th century, and is an example of the historical accuracy of the reconstructed landscape. Although it can be said that the gardens at Williamsburg are merely reconstructions, there would be very few of the original plants, if any, existing today if there had been no break in continuity up to the present time.*

attempts to preserve the historical phases of a churchyard have kept the best gravestones from each period *in situ*, with due account of local notabilities, and arranged some of the less important stones against the boundary walls or in the paved areas, while those of little importance and poor in visual quality have been buried (when there has been no response to the statutory procedure of giving due notice of the intention).

In making the decision about the date at which the conservation policy should be aimed or whether several dates appertaining to different parts of the landscape should be the policy, several matters will need to be considered, such as the rarity of particular examples in the region and even in the country, the need to keep or bring back the landscape associated with the buildings or artefacts, the aesthetic value of

the landscape at different periods, and the initial costs and future maintenance costs. Today, the interest in the ecology of the landscape will more likely affect the conservation of large rural landscapes than of the designed gardens. There are many people who are strong in support of so-called wild or natural landscape when, in fact, if human influence was removed, the basic ecology – founded upon the geology, the

2.4 *The churchyard of the mediaeval parish church of Darlington Co. Durham. Over the years this churchyard had become filled with gravestones and dense planting typical of the 19th century. The work shown in this illustration aimed to bring back the earlier more open appearance of the setting of the church, but retained examples of the different types of gravestones. There is also the advantage that the churchyard can now serve as an accessible quiet place in the midst of a busy town. (Landscape architects: B. Hackett and B. Robson.)*

climate and a gradual return to something like the original soil type – would prevail and in most situations bring back the true landscape; a classic example is the Lüneberg Heide in West Germany where the beautiful heather and juniper landscape requires conservation techniques to prevent it reverting to a birch forest, and subsequently to some form of high forest, for example, controlling the birch seedlings by sheep grazing.[1] A similar dilemma occurs when afforestation is proposed on open moorland in Britain because the conservation of the true natural landscape would mean closing down the sheep grazing and allowing the sparse forest to re-assert itself. On the other hand, by setting a date in history when grazing was most successful, one can argue conservation on the basis of the historical interest in the long-standing practice of sheep grazing.

The true history of a landscape is one of change; if we, today, 'freeze' a landscape to a particular period in history, how will future generations consider a landscape which has not responded to changing historical events? And landscape conservation is concerned with a 'living' landscape which is not in sympathy with a 'frozen' landscape. The Countryside Review Committee's discussion paper on 'The Countryside – Problems and Policies' has this to say on the conservation issue: 'Conservation essentially implies respect: respect for the natural resources of our countryside – whether visual, ecological or economic. It is therefore an ethic, as well as a code of practice. It demands policies geared towards long-term equilibrium – an awareness of man's potential harmony with his surroundings, not an acquiescence in their destruction – nor, on the other hand, a determination to freeze the current scene. For above all, the word should signify a dynamic process, one which incorporates, indeed depends on, change. The term has been abused and devalued. It should not be equated with preserving, unchanged, landscapes, species, buildings, and monuments.'[2] These admirable words while fully applicable to landscape generally, cannot be applied without qualification to the safeguarding of historic landscape where there is a particular date to be kept in mind.

Conservation, if it is to accord with the dynamic quality of landscape and with a changing civilization, must have as its objective the combining of preservation and development in those areas inhabited by people. There will be people who want no change, and people whose only interest is increasing the earning power of the landscape and adjusting it to accommodate the new machines that speed the pace of living. If the landscape is in small ownerships, people with these diverse interests have to be won over to a policy which safeguards the heritage landscape, and conserves the rest in a way that brings back its natural fertility where this has been allowed to decline, and maintains its natural fertility where changes are to be made. If the landscape is in a large single ownership, the heritage interest is usually greater, but at greater risk because of the tax inroads that short-sighted governments make for the cost of maintaining a heritage landscape.

Whether landscape is in many small ownerships or a large single ownership makes no difference to the fact that landscape only respects its own ecological boundaries within the original natural landscape, and these are not screening boundaries in the accepted sense; unless a determined attempt is made to screen a particular landscape at the ownership boundary from public view, its preservation and development are the concern of more people than its owners. There is a good tradition among landowners of large estates to share the beauty of their landscapes with the population at large; without the large single ownerships many more landscapes would have been split up into diverse properties. It is a political argument which has been debated time and time again, but you cannot overlook the fact that much fine landscape, worthy of both preservation and development, has been split up into numerous properties of little environmental distinction as a result of heavy taxation.

When action takes place from a Central Government decision to set up large single ownerships under public bodies, the responsible Ministers and the public bodies under them in Britain are required to 'have regard to the desirability of conserving the natural beauty and amenity of the countryside',[3] although it would more likely be translated into action if they were also required to produce regularly and in public a report on the nature and extent of this 'regard' – as suggested by the Countryside Review Committee set up by the Secretary of State for the Environment in 1974.[4]

The involvement of the public with landscape, apart from enjoying its appearance from a distance, raises the problem of use and access. When the fertility status of the landscape and its appearance depend upon the way it is used, over-use or a change of use will lead to deterioration or a change in appearance. A

2.5   *An example of eroded agricultural land in Israel, due to incorrect soil conservation measures and over-use.*

type of farming which uses the same techniques year in and year out in a way that maintains the fertility status of the landscape will keep its appearance, but new methods or over-use will change the appearance. With the recreational use of landscape by the public, over-use can damage the very thing they come to see and enjoy. Thus, conservation has the dilemma of having to apply limits to the pleasure it seeks to provide. The solution suggested by the Countryside Commission is by 'on site' and 'day-to-day' management (see Chapter Five). The National Trust has this problem in its properties, and has decided that protection must have priority over use and access, but the Trust is charged with the duty of preserving landscape and buildings 'for the nation's use and enjoyment'[5], which means holding a fine balance between restricting access and use, and keeping landscapes and buildings in a good state of preservation.

In densely populated countries, it is natural that the lobby for recreation facilities in the countryside should try to find a solution to the problem of access by the recreation seeker to farmland which has retained the trees and hedgerows of some enclosure movement, and has an attractive appearance. Interference with the farming operations is the landowner's concern, rather than disallowing anyone to enjoy his rural landscape. Professor Gerald Wibberley and Dr Bryn Green of the Countryside Planning Unit, Wye College in the University of London, told planners at a meeting in 1978 that it was proving increasingly difficult to have real multiple use of the countryside and that the farmer could no longer be expected to be the nation's unpaid landscape gardener. One possible contribution to solving the demand for recreational access and retaining the rural landscapes of the past would be to make up for any reduction in agricultural production in areas of British land farmed under older traditional methods from the extensive farming on the Continent. Surely in practice as well as in theory, the rural land resources of the European Economic Community should be used in an European manner rather than each individual country concentrating on increasing its national self-sufficiency in food.

We also have to draw the line between people

2.6 *An agricultural area in the east Netherlands where parts of the hedgerows have been preserved whilst opening out the landscape for use by modern machines. This kind of modification of the landscape and new agricultural methods does not radically alter the appearance and does not act to produce a decline in fertility.*

having unlimited access to historic and other landscapes which are under some form of conservation protection, and very restricted access in order that a visitor can experience the quiet of the historic period. Otherwise, the proximity of many people, cars, tractors and airplanes – to say nothing of transistor radios – deprives the visitor of the complete experience offered by these landscapes. However, in France especially many historic formal gardens come alive when there are plenty of people moving around, because they were designed for a great number of guests and courtiers.

Reading back through this Chapter, it is apparent that if these several dilemmas are to be resolved so that future generations will thank us for what we have handed on, landscape conservation must be itself a design and planning process, requiring as much

professional skill and balanced lay decision-making as the design and planning of a new landscape development.

[1]See also Charlton, P., and Stiles, R., *'Conservation, Lüneberg Heath, Germany'*, in *Landscape Design*, No. 124 (London, 1978).
[2]Countryside Review Committee, *Discussion paper on The Countryside – Problems and Policies*, paras. 45 & 46 (HMSO 1976), Quoted by permission of the Controller.
[3]The Countryside Act, 1968, Section 11, HMSO.
[4]See note 2, para. 61.
[5]*The National Trust: Conservation and Access* (The National Trust: London, 1973).

Overleaf

2.7 *This engraving of the Tuileries Gardens in Paris at the time when high society took part in large scale entertainments shows the ample provision made for large crowds. If the images of the people were removed from this engraving, the landscape would lack some of its interest. However, not all historic and other landscapes were designed to accept large numbers of people, and in such cases the problems of public access have to be faced.*

Chapter 3

Decision making

Where a landscape has a special scientific interest, such as the habitat of a rare species or an exposed geological formation of considerable educational value, we can usually rely upon the scientists, represented in Britain by the several Institutes and Associations of the Natural Environmental Research Council, the Nature Conservancy Council and the Institute of Geological Sciences, to identify it and plan for its conservation. There are other landscapes considered by many people to be 'wild' or 'natural' and about which decisions have to be made on amenity rather than scientific grounds. Some of these landscapes are not entirely natural, and are in a state of reversion to a natural landscape after the cessation of some activity of man; an example is the Shenandoah National Park in the USA which has been allowed to revert to natural forest after its short life as farmland. But this Park raises the question whether some of the land should be kept in a farmland state as an historical record, or whether there is a particular quality in a landscape where nature absorbs a past human activity into her way of reclaiming landscape, and this quality may differ in some respects from the original natural landscape. There is, of course, another conservation principle which incorporates the moral obligation to nature to go beyond merely stopping the human activity, and in addition sets up processes which will assist nature to reclaim the original natural landscape in all respects; examples are some desert landscapes which are unable to bring back the original vegetation after over-grazing and tree and shrub removal unless some outside assistance is brought in.

There is no easy answer to the decision whether or not preservation measures preventing any change to a landscape, or conservation measures allowing change with the maintenance of fertility should be applied to a landscape. Many of the principles and factors mentioned in these Chapters will need to be reviewed by all those able to influence planning decisions to see how relevant they are to any landscape which is subject to development proposals or which may be in danger of changing through neglect.

Professor Albert Fein has drawn attention to the conservation principle that was recommended for Niagara Falls, when the question of stabilizing their present form arose because the Falls were in danger of receding.[1] The group of experts, who were consulted, recommended that there should be no intervention in the natural processes of change, even though the appearance every one knows might in time become different. The group did, however, recommend that a study should be made of the whole river system, which might produce another solution to the future of the Falls; this draws attention to the need to look at areas which are on the list for conservation in the context of the natural landscape unit of which they form a part and also in relation to the changes wrought by man in the surrounding area.

In the previous Chapter we looked at the problems raised by public access to landscapes which are scheduled or listed for conservation; it is such an important matter that we ought to consider further how landscapes react to access by large numbers of people.

In order to avoid interference with natural and 'wild' landscapes, access arrangements for the general public will require a different approach than with designed landscapes. In the former landscapes, wear and tear is most evident in the places where people congregate through habit or where 'natural' routes meet. These may not represent the kind of footpath plan which would produce the least damage to the landscape; it may prove too late to stop an established custom, and to construct a footpath system may be contrary to the character of the landscape. Somehow, the number of visitors needs to be reduced or they must be drawn away from the areas at risk.

Restricting access to publicly-owned natural landscapes raises difficulties, but to quote Professor Fein again, there is, according to some reputable

3.1 *Some of the forest areas of the Shenandoah National Park in the USA were farmland until the more profitable Mid West was opened up. This illustration shows an example of the original pasture land which is kept in this form for historical interest.*

authorities, a sound moral reason why 'natural objects' should have rights under the law, as well as our rights as human beings. If this principle is accepted, a restriction on use by the general public is fair in order that the right of the landscape to survive is upheld. As it happens, the exposed rock areas of mountains are better able to withstand the wear and tear of visitors, compared with lush landscapes, but are the least used; reference should be made, however, to scree areas where vegetation among the broken rocks is at risk from wear and tear. If we are to get across to people the fact that natural landscapes must be used cautiously if they are not to be upset, a twofold approach to them should be made which spells out the ecological imbalance of too many people and the equal right of all living beings to have access to and

live in and be part of natural landscapes. This approach is more relevant today than concentrating solely on damage by people, and it follows that landscape conservation needs to be accompanied by a parallel policy of education about nature and its sensitivity to imbalance, and by people having a responsible attitude in this respect.

Education and a social conscience can do more than persuade people to fall in with a conservation plan, because they can also lead to people pressing governments and responsible bodies to be more active in conservation measures. Sadly, it often requires the effect of over-use by visitors to bring the need for conservation measures to the fore. John Bailey, Chairman of the National Trust from 1923 to 1931, gave as a conservation principle in relation to access, that 'Preservation may always permit of access, while without preservation access becomes forever impossible.' For the National Parks, a directive was issued in a Circular from the Department of the Environment to the effect that where recreation pressures are in conflict with landscape conservation, the latter should have priority.

Many historic landscapes, particularly those resulting from economic land uses, require the associated activities to continue, otherwise their true historical character is missing: an elaborate formal garden,

3.2 *An experimental scheme to cultivate the desert land at Avdat in Israel, using methods practised many centuries ago, including the gathering and directing of the limited rainfall to the new agricultural area.*

32

3.3 *These terraced rice fields in Japan not only have considerable landscape interest through the way they relate to the natural topography, but they represent a way of life and a method of cultivation which may well pass into history unless special arrangements can be made to overcome the gap between the present high cost of labour and the market price of the commodity.*

particularly the French examples mentioned previously, does not exhibit its true landscape character without many people using it; terraced rice fields in the Far East on a steep hillside need hand labour rather than machines to keep them as they were originally laid out. With these and other examples in mind, a conservation principle which should often be adopted is to associate use with a conservation plan, and the closer the methods and techniques of the use are to the original ones, the more likely is the landscape to keep its particular qualities.

When planning authorities, amenity societies and other groups concerned about conservation have to make a decision whether they will initiate action over the safeguarding of some historic landscape, it will assist their deliberations if they consider how certain principles may be applicable as well as reviewing the

many land-use, economic and ownership matters. It is to be hoped that an official body will have already made a list or inventory of those landscapes which might conceivably have a claim for safeguarding. When it comes to taking action, which may involve compensation and other difficulties, if there is a proposal to radically change the landscape, the following matters rank as principles upon which a case for safeguarding might be based:

1. The intrinsic value of the landscape as regards its appearance and pleasurable qualities — this should be relative to other landscapes in the locality or region because what may rank as average quality landscape in one area may be regarded as good in an area of generally poor quality landscape. The quality of a landscape is often a major factor in gaining support for its protection.

2. Historical rarity — it will be recalled that, as a minimum, an example of each period and type of historic landscape should be protected in a country. This should be followed by a similar protection at the regional and local levels, although at these levels gaps are likely to occur. Upon this comprehensive basis, although small in number, the cultural heritage of a

3.4 *Examples of small historical gardens can be seen at Williamsburg, USA, although these have been reconstructed from research. Small historical gardens which have retained their original form are less frequent than the larger gardens, possibly because they were easier to change and subsequent owners were unlikely to have a long history of the same family behind them which would influence them to preserve their past.*

country can only benefit if additions are made to the number of landscapes safeguarded or conserved.

3. Historical interest – a landscape may not have a special visual appeal, yet it may have important connotations with some historical event, such as the site of a famous battle. There are also the sites of archaeological interest, but with no special visual appeal.

4. Environmental quality – not to be confused with intrinsic value as regards appearance and pleasurable qualities, and concerned more with those older urban areas where the green landscape is dominant and there is shelter, sunshine and a human scale. The safeguarding of these areas is not only important for their intrinsic value, historical rarity and interest, but to prevent something taking its place which would have a difficult task equalling the original with the current standard of urban development.

At some time, the preparation of a list or inventory, and the subsequent decision-making stage whether or not to ensure safeguarding or conservation, will present the authority concerned with the problem of what to do about gaps in the history of the landscape. The gaps are more likely to result from a change from an old to a new style, with the loss of the old style, than from the fact that no development was made to any landscape in one or more periods. Is a restoration of the missing phase justified when the replacement landscape is beautiful and in good health? – a point made previously with regard to the examples of the 18th-century English School of Landscape which replaced a great many 17th-century formal gardens. In addition to the four principles outlined, the following matters should be taken into account at the decision-making stage: the amount of evidence available on the layout and appearance of the earlier landscape; the contribution made by the existing landscape as a setting for buildings of architectural quality – replacement by an earlier landscape style might not accord with these buildings; and the possibly prohibitive costs of carrying out the replacement.

Somehow we associate conserving landscapes with examples which are large in area. This may be so because the larger area is likely to be accompanied by greater opportunities for revenue, and there is a tendency to assume that small areas can be handled by their owners without outside assistance from grants or visitor revenue. Nevertheless, the small examples of historic landscape are just as much a part of a nation's cultural heritage as the large examples. There are few, if any, small urban gardens in the larger cities which remain as they were laid out at the time the houses were built, and this is where restoration of the kind practised in small properties in Williamsburg in the USA is justified in a few examples.

Interest in the small historic gardens in cities and in ancient cultivation practices in the countryside has also been over-shadowed by interest in those large landscapes whose traditional appearance depends upon the scale of traditional agricultural and forestry practices which are no longer economic or acceptable to the present-day worker in agriculture and forestry. At least, keeping a few examples of the mediaeval open field pattern, and restoring the fields of a Roman villa settlement are just as important to a nation's cultural heritage as the conservation of the enclosed fields and historic gardens and parklands. But the conservation of historic examples of agriculture and forestry, and particularly of the former, means setting up the necessary organization to cultivate them, because there is unlikely to be a financial return from visitors and only a small one from a form of cultivation which will not match the prevailing return from modern methods. Associating these examples with a folk or industrial museum as a nucleus was a proposal made at the International Symposium for the Safeguarding of Historic Landscape held in Japan in 1977 with regard to a small area of traditional rice cultivation in the suburbs of Kyoto.

There are advantages in a landscape scheduled for conservation remaining under the control, or partial control, of the owner, because he or she will have knowledge that is invaluable when maintenance and restoration plans are formulated. The Management Plan for the Upton Castle Estate (Pembroke Dock, County Dyfed, Wales) emphasizes this point: 'it is felt that the expertise and intimate knowledge of the Estate which the owners possess should be sought and utilized to carry out the plan itself, and that this can be augmented and increased by drawing upon the resources of the National Park Department.'[2]

The decision to seek protection for a landscape of special wildlife interest will be influenced by the advice of the scientist who may draw attention to its unique position as a rare habitat for some species or an essential transitory habitat for migrating birds. This advice can be complicated if the site also has visual or historic interest which may, on the one hand, strengthen the case for conservation, but, on the other hand, weaken it because there will be resistance to access by people seeking the visual pleasure and historic interest. The conservation of landscapes with special scientific interest is, however, better provided in Britain than with the historic landscapes, because the Nature Conservancy Council, for example, has an organization which can undertake practical conservation, whereas there is not a similar national body for historic landscapes, except where the landscape is the setting for a scheduled ancient monument under the care of the appropriate section of the Department of the Environment, although National Park authorities do carry out practical conservation where possible in the Parks.

Vegetation is essential to the appearance of most historic landscapes, but, unlike the long life of ancient monuments when properly cared for, the life of trees and shrubs is limited. Thus, in an historic landscape, while many of the trees planted when it was developed may still be alive though near the end of life, most of the shrubs and other plants will have been replaced, often with different species (see also page 18). The faithful historian will try to find out the species originally planted, but even so, many of them may not be available today, or would succumb to a disease. How are proper decisions to be made with the planting? As a matter of principle, the structural planting usually effected by the trees is more important to retain and replant as necessary in its original form. With the smaller plants, the first step, failing exact replacement, would be to substitute plants in contemporary use which are not too dissimilar in appearance. In fact, in historical times, it is safe to assume that the smaller plants were changed from time to time, just as they are changed today.

In Britain, provision is made in the planning legislation for preventing the removal of trees which are particularly important in the appearance of an environment. But, again on this point that vegetation has a limited life, John Workman, advisor on conservation and forestry to the National Trust, has drawn attention to the use of the term 'Preservation Order' which may be appropriate for buildings, but is inappropriate for trees which cannot be kept in exactly the state they were in at the date of an Order, being subject to death from old age or disease. He suggests the term 'Conservation Order' as a more accurate term, which suggests that a tree should be nurtured, if necessary, with fertilizers, the maintenance of proper drainage, tree surgery and other operations of a caring kind. In the same paper,[3] John Workman suggested a principle with reference to trees to guide one in conservation

decisions which could well be followed: 'My job is to ensure that those who tour England in two hundred years' time, when none of the actual trees planted in the eighteenth century survive, will still be able to distinguish between examples of Brown and Repton and see on the gound the interpretation of those masters of design who themselves never saw the fulfiment of their work.' A good principle to follow, and perhaps we, in planning conservation, should always look years ahead to speculate how our conservation practices will have kept alive the examples which are classified as 'of historic interest'.

3.5 *Soudley Ponds in the Forest of Dean. In this view the conifers take their place in a visually acceptable manner in the landscape, while the presence of areas of deciduous trees help considerably in this respect. The well known controversy over deciduous versus coniferous planting in Britain loses some of its edge when an afforestation plan producing the kind of landscape seen in this illustration has been drawn up. (Courtesy of the Forestry Commission)*

The familiar argument whether it is admissible on landscape planning principles to plant conifers in a deciduous tree environment has occurred with many landscapes for which afforestation proposals have been made. As early as 1810, when William Wordsworth's *Guide to England's Lake District* was published, the visual problems of conifers in naturally deciduous landscapes have been recognized. On the other side of the coin is the contention that to put back a forest where it once existed, even if the kinds of tree are different, is no worse than maintaining a landscape kept open by sheep grazing. Conifers versus deciduous trees is an argument typical of many that will enter into decision-making on conservation matters. There are, of course, compromises where sympathetic planning of a new forest can retain the best views, arrange forest edges to accord with the topography, and where planting some deciduous species intermingling with the conifers will produce an acceptable landscape. All this is symptomatic of the skill and clear thinking required in conservation work in landscapes under economic and recreational pressures. These and many other solutions to the problem of conifers versus deciduous trees have been seen in recent years as a result of Dame Sylvia Crowe's landscape advisory services to the Forestry Commission, and were put forward by the author in a paper in 1949.[4]

[1] Fein, Albert *Basic Ideas and Principles for the Safeguarding of Historic Landscapes, Report of the International Symposium of Experts for the Safeguarding of Historic Landscape* (Tokyo, 1977).
[2] Wheeler, N. J., *Upton Castle Management Plan* (National Parks Department, Pembrokeshire Coast, Haverfordwest, 1975).
[3] Workman, John, *Trees in the Designed Landscape Setting*, Garden History Society Symposium papers (1975).
[4] Hackett, Brian, 'Design in Rural Landscape', in *Planning Outlook*, (Oxford University Press, 1949).

Chapter 4

Keeping a record

Without the knowledge of a nation's total landscape assets, a representative list of landscapes deemed worthy of, or needing conservation cannot be properly compiled. The task of preparing such a list is very large, but in England the interest shown by the Council for the Protection of Rural England and its branches in helping to prepare lists of historic landscapes and specially beautiful areas is an example of the possibility of mustering volunteers for this time-consuming and foot-slogging work; it is thus made possible for planning authorities, as presently staffed, to cope with preparing comprehensive lists. In fact, the policy of a planning authority for landscape conservation should have as priority the preparation of an inventory of the landscapes in its area, including those of historic, scientific, and amenity interest – the latter also including the specially beautiful and those with recreational potential. These categories can be sub-divided to note a special cultural, social, recreational, or economic significance, and again each landscape in the list can be noted as requiring or not, as the case may be, replanting or repair works.

There is, of course, a strong case for identifying areas for conservation as with the national heritage inventory of Eire[1] and, one hopes, for being able to apply conservation measures to the greater part of the landscape of most countries; this could lead to high compensation costs and discourage creative landscape development to meet the changing circumstances as the years pass by. A comprehensive planning control of the landscape would, however, be able to handle both the conservation and the development aspects, provided the legislation is adequate and the planning authority staffed with the required

number of persons trained in landscape to evaluate the effect of development proposals upon the landscape. They would also be needed to identify elements worthy of conservation which lie within areas of development, such as fine trees, streams and favourable habitats.

The emphasis on listing and scheduling has been on buildings rather than on landscapes, despite the fact that externally a building has no significance unless there is landscape around it which enables it to be seen, and, in many examples, enhances the appearance of the building. Landscapes have come a poor second best in listing in Britain, although planning authorities in their statutory survey work have noted areas of outstanding beauty and of historic interest. But it is unlikely that any planning authority or voluntary organization can have studied the landscape of their area with the same degree of thoroughness that J. St. Bodfan Gruffydd employed for his survey in Oxfordshire, North of the Thames, of historic gardens and parks.[2] His report suggested a method for recording areas of historic landscape which included the location, designer (if known), the kind of landscape, its physical characteristics, design character, condition, access, etc.; these details were appended to the record of each site which would be grouped under the types of landscape quoted in Chapter One. Aided by voluntary organizations, it should be possible for planning authorities to produce landscape inventories of all the classes and kinds of landscape which have a claim to be conserved. The task of identifying landscapes for conservation is more difficult than with buildings which are compact elements and quickly seen to have or not to have quality and interest; thus, voluntary help is likely to be the only way planning authorities, as currently staffed, can accomplish the preparation of a list for submission to the Central Government department who will have the final say.

At the level of Central Government bodies in Britain, various landscapes have been scheduled and are thus on a list for safeguarding and conservation, with varying degrees of restoration and maintenance. Examples are the archaeological sites under the Ancient Monuments and Historic Areas Conservation Division of the Department of the Environment, the

National and the Countryside Parks and Heritage Coasts for which the Countryside Commission holds a 'watching brief' and makes grants, and the National

4.1 A plan (not dated), but probably near the end of the 18th century, of farmland at Matfen in Northumberland. Old estate maps, such as this example, disclose valuable information for making a case for the conservation of a landscape when its historical interest adds to the aesthetic interest. Also, these estate maps provide information about hedgerows and woodlands which might be replanted as part of a conservation programme. (Courtesy of Hugh Blackett and the Northumberland County Archivist)

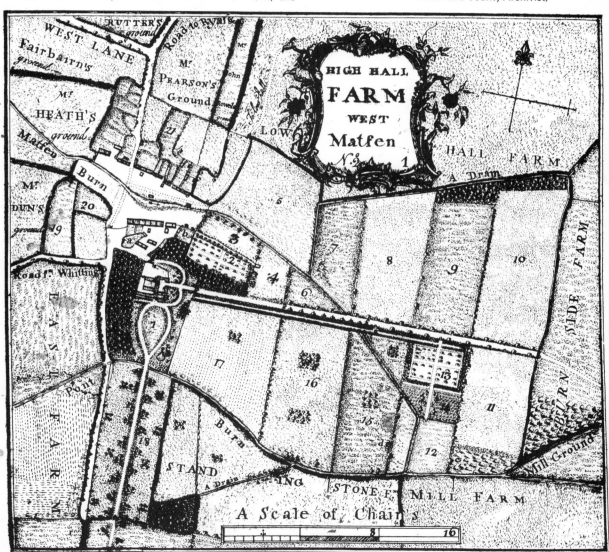

Nature Reserves and Sites of Special Scientific Interest of the Nature Conservancy Council. These landscapes enjoy some measure of protection which varies in accordance with the statutory position[3], but there is a far greater number of merit which are not on any 'statutory list' and have conservation policies ranging from the non-existent to the adequate. As a first and essential step towards conservation, these landscapes should be identified and listed as J. St Bodfan Gruffydd suggests.

Deciding which landscapes might be considered for listing, and into which class and kind, should be based upon research into their history and ownership and upon the opinion of those carrying out the survey, possibly checked by a review committee. Deciding which of these landscapes eventually qualify to be put on a statutory list can be helped by considering the four principles suggested in Chapter Three for historic landscapes as an aid to considering whether or not to take positive action to safeguard a landscape.

Before ranging over the landscape to identify landscapes for possible listing, there are preliminary investigations which can narrow down the number of miles tramped or traversed by vehicle. The following sources will prove helpful:

1. Ordnance Survey and Land Utilization Survey maps, estate maps, and air photographic coverage.

2. Organizations who may have carried out landscape surveys, such as planning authorities, relevant University and Polytechnic Departments, etc.

3. Old books on the area, including local histories and biographies of landscape designers and landowners.

4. Knowledgeable persons, such as landowners from long-established families and county archivists, local amenity, historical, archaeological and architectural societies, natural history societies, and organizations like the Country Landowners' Association, the Royal Forestry Society, the National Farmers' Union, the Council for the Protection of Rural England. Although the National Trust is already involved in safeguarding properties, it will be aware of properties about which it has been approached, but unable to negotiate further.

There would be every advantage if the landowners concerned could agree with, and welcome the listing of their landscapes, but this would be more likely to happen if there were proper financial aids through grants and, more essential, tax relief — the latter being a continuing aid which is necessary because of continuing maintenance. This kind of recognition by grants and tax relief of the job landowners undertake

in husbanding one of a nation's most valuable resources would help to remove the problem of access for the purpose of identifying landscapes qualifying for listing; with this assistance legislation would not be amiss and could enable access to take place in the same way that a planning authority can gain access to land for carrying out its statutory investigations, but how much better for all concerned if the landowner can be helpful, even to the point of hoping his landscape will be listed.

Some areas of landscape which might qualify for listing comprise numerous ownerships, several different uses, and buildings here and there. In these cases, the 'conservation area' approach is a good solution, because scheduling such an area by statute can mean that development proposals are strictly controlled over the changes they might bring to the area, and alterations like felling trees or replacing a thatched roof by a tiled roof would have to be approved. The UNESCO recommendations made in Paris in 1962 included the scheduling of extensive landscapes 'by zones' as one of the methods of safeguarding landscapes.[4]

During the investigations and survey work to produce a list for the selection of landscapes scheduled for safeguarding, the provenance of some landscapes may be in doubt, particularly when the interest lies in ancient times. If reconstruction works will be necessary to make the landscape sufficiently interesting to justify scheduling for safeguarding, expenditure of public funds, and bringing in visitors, it may require the help of scientists. For example, in order to give an accurate appearance to the reconstructed landscape, the new planting should be as close as possible to that in evidence perhaps hundreds of years ago.[5] When the reconstruction is to a period many hundreds of years ago, scientific methods now available can help to date the remains of vegetation by pollen, carbon and charcoal analysis, when the conditions are suitable — for example, an undisturbed site with a high water table which may have allowed incompletely decomposed vegetation to retain the original pollen in an identifiable state. Relating the pollen to the different levels in the soil helps to date the vegetation, but even with the undisturbed sites, cultivation practices in the past tend to mix the soil at different levels and confuse the dating, also some pollen from weed species is difficult to distinguish from the pollen of cultivated plants. Another difficulty met by the scientist is that charcoal analysis requires a fire to have occurred at a known date, and it is sometimes difficult to identify species when the charcoal remains are in very small pieces. All these investigations are expensive and it may only be possible to schedule the site to preserve it from interference rather than as a quality landscape with historic interest whose provenance has yet to be determined through scientific and excavation techniques.

The case for including rural landscapes in a list for conservation sometimes depends as much upon historical interest and rarity as upon appearance, but to make a strong case will require evidence about the dating of hedgerows and woodlands, and about the layout of the fields in relation to earlier cultivation practices. There is now an increasing number of experts interested in the use of scientific methods for identifying landscapes in relation to dates when they were laid out in a certain manner. Also, the growing interest in local history brings to light information on the details of the landscape.

Scientists and historians can produce the factual evidence to support the historical interest of a landscape, but factual evidence to support the value of the appearance of a landscape is not easily produced. There may be the praise of some well known person who has immortalized the landscape in his writings, or the landscape has become accepted as particularly beautiful through the transmission of opinion from one generation to another. Many attempts have been made to produce evaluation techniques which measure the appearance value of landscape, some depending entirely upon measuring elements, others upon visual assessment by qualified persons, and still others combining both measurement and observation. The University of Manchester project, sponsored by the Countryside Commission, is among an increasing number of publications which examine existing techniques and make proposals for new ones for landscape evaluation.[6] While the emphasis in listing is on rarity, special beauty and considerable historical interest, selection without sophisticated landscape evaluation is not difficult. But if listing becomes more general, or much supporting evidence has to be produced to persuade the deciding authority that listing a particular landscape is justified, these landscape evaluation methods are likely to be helpful.

The evaluation of landscape quality on a basis that might be universally acceptable is difficult enough. More so, and usually impossible, is a monetary evaluation of loss or gain with a landscape subject to conservation measures. It is possible to cost a changeover from the traditional management of an estate to a management plan for profitable recreation, but even so, the gain in working capacity and health of the visitors from the pleasure of visiting the estate would not be measurable. Property values, which might increase after scheduling a particular adjoining area of landscape for conservation, could sometimes be used as an indication of the financial benefits. But the subject is a difficult one and the hope is that people will realize that the best things are beyond price.

[1]The National Institute for Physical Planning and Construction Research, *National Heritage Inventory (Landscape section),* An Foras Forbartha, St Martin's House, Waterloo Rd, Dublin.
[2]See Chapter One, note 4.
[3]See Cherry, G. E., *'The Conservation Movement',* Journal of the Royal Town Planning Institute (London, January 1975).
[4]UNESCO, *Recommendation concerning the safeguarding of the beauty and character of landscapes and sites* (Paris, 1962).
[5]Dimbleby, G. W., *'Pollen as Botanical Evidence of the past, Landscape Architecture* (USA, May 1976), pp. 219–23.
[6]*The Landscape Evaluation Research Project 1970–75* (University of Manchester, 1976).

Overleaf

4.2 *A landscape plan by J. Robson, dated 1792, for the improvement of the parkland around Belsay Castle in Northumberland. Many of the proposals were not carried out, such as the long lake, but the fact that the plan was commissioned indicates the great interest of the landowner which eventually led to landscape works of great beauty and historical interest. The existence of the plan is also one matter which should be taken into account by anyone scheduling landscapes for conservation. (Courtesy of Sir Stephen Middleton Bart. and the Northumberland County Archivist)*

Chapter 5

Conservation in the countryside

Landscape conservation involves three stages, of which the first two — finding out what needs to be conserved and deciding what is possible to conserve— have been considered in previous Chapters. The third stage is the practical one when listing and scheduling lead to work on the ground, the method of achieving conservation being the first step, followed by the establishment of an organization for maintenance or continuing use. UNESCO in the 1962 Recommendations[1] suggested six methods which might be adopted for the 'safeguarding of landscapes and sites':

1. General supervision by the responsible authorities.
2. Insertion of obligations into urban development plans and planning at all levels: regional, rural and urban.
3. Scheduling of extensive landscapes 'by zones'.
4. Scheduling of isolated sites.
5. Creation and maintenance of natural reserves and national parks.
6. Acquisition of sites by communities.

These six methods are explained in some detail in the Recommendations, and are followed by recommendations for the application of protective measures which briefly state that landscape conservation should have 'the force of law', and should have specialized bodies of an administrative or advisory nature; some British planning authorities have now established their own urban conservation sections in line with the latter recommendation.

But, considering landscapes in the countryside, the areas are usually large and the appearance for the most part results from the land uses, so that the detailed control applied when a building or a garden is scheduled for conservation on historic or appearance grounds is hardly possible. There are sometimes small areas of considerable importance where the relic of an ancient forest or the layout of an old farming system remains, and the objective could be to protect against any change with perhaps some reconstruction, in the second example, of parts of ditches and terraces which have disappeared. The best solution for the conservation of these small areas is that they should be acquired and placed under a trust or public ownership unless the landowner is given financial assistance, because they will need to be managed under forestry and farming methods which are not sufficiently profitable today. In areas which are less significant historically, three conservation policies can be suggested: first, a legal requirement upon the owner, such as a preservation order; second, a financial incentive to the owner; third, co-operating with a willing landowner and his tenant. The first policy is unlikely to be successful without financial aid because many excuses can be made why the vegetation died or erosion set in, all apparently beyond the control of the owner; it might be possible to achieve the objective by placing only key elements like trees and hedgerows under a preservation order. The second policy is more likely to be successful if the financial incentive covers

5.1 *These two plans of farmland at Poringland, in South Norfolk, show the decline in hedgerow and field pattern between 1946 (above) and 1973 (below). The Norfolk County Council has, however, instituted a scheme, supported by Countryside Commission grants, whereby a specific rural area is chosen each year and each landowner and farmer is asked to co-operate in a replanting scheme. More than two thirds of those approached have been willing to co-operate. (Courtesy of the Norfolk County Planning Department)*

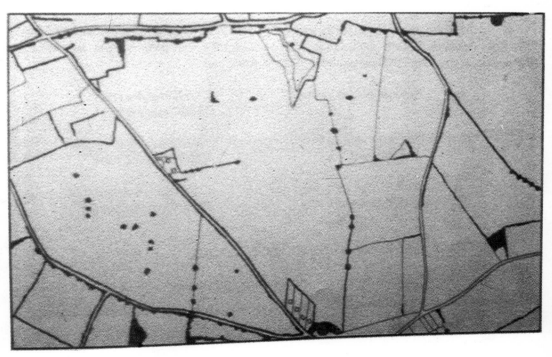

both the cost of maintaining the landscape and compensation for the likely diminished income, but governments have not been generous in this way. The third policy can be successful if the landowner is not dependent upon the income from the land in question, but he or she will need to be convinced of the historical or visual interest, particularly its rarity, before agreeing to what may be a sacrifice of some of their potential income.

The greater part of the countryside has landscapes which have changed through the ages with different agricultural and afforestation methods and, apart from keeping small areas as an historical record, it would be unrealistic to try and prevent further changes and thus act contrary to history which is a story of change. But the argument in support of change to the greater part of the rural landscape should be qualified by asking whether a proposed change will have long-term benefit, whether it is likely to reduce the natural fertility of the landscape, and whether it will interfere with the layout where this is already well arranged for improving the microclimate and gives a flexibility for the particular land use. At the same time, a proposed change to a landscape with visual interest from the

pattern of trees, hedges and fields should require these questions to be answered very convincingly before the functional and much admired rural landscapes of Britain, for example, are swept aside for a windswept open landscape. While agricultural and afforestation land is for the most part exempt from planning control, these are not questions which will be asked at a public inquiry, but opposition can be influential – the more so, if it is responsible and has considered these questions before entering the lists of informal criticism of a proposal for change. Pending the day when perhaps all land uses (including Crown lands) are subject to democratic planning control, some interim surveillance over what is happening to the rural landscape is an urgent matter. The Council for the Protection of Rural England in commenting in 1975 upon the study commissioned by the Countryside Commission – New Agricultural Landscapes[2] – suggested an 'early warning system' of

5.2   *Although these hedgerow trees have been allowed to survive, their future is obviously limited in view of their age and condition. A constant programme of hedgerow replanting should be part of a conservation scheme for a rural area. (Courtesy of the Norfolk County Planning Department)*

impending landscape changes in the countryside would be a wise interim measure. With this proposal landowners and tenants in the countryside would be under a legal obligation to give notice of their intention to change the character of the landscape of land they owned or managed; for example, if they planned to remove a well-established hedge, or change upland grazing land into forest or arable land. The merit of this proposal is that it would give time and the opportunity

for representations to be made to the landowner or

5.3   *One of the lanes in the countryside of Essex, for which the County Planning Department has a policy to place them under protective measures. With the growth of visitor traffic and the increase in size of farm vehicles, it is important that, at least, some of these delightful elements of the landscape should be conserved, particularly as they often vary in character from one region to another. (Courtesy of the Essex County Planning Department)*

tenant, and to any government department likely to be approached for grant assistance for the change of use, persuasion sometimes being as effective as the law. The Advisory Council for Agriculture and Horticulture received the suggestion of a statutory early warning system when the Minister for Agriculture, Fisheries and Food asked the Council to look into ways of reconciling production and conservation and amenity in the countryside;[3] but this was not accepted, the Council preferring voluntary action by farmers over conservation. The anomalous position regarding the conservation of the rural landscape is that while trees can be subject to preservation orders, there is no similar protection for hedgerows which are often more essential to the landscape of Britain than isolated trees.

Countryside management is a method of resolving some of the conflicts that arise between the interests of the landowner or tenant and those of conservation. This method has been developed by the Countryside Commission and depends upon informal negotiation by a project or management officer, appointed by the Commission, who will live on the job and who should not be connected with any formal or statutory control of land use, although he should be in contact with the planning authority and the local or regional staff of agricultural and forestry bodies. His personal qualities are the key to the success of countryside management, and he should have access to some direct financial support for small projects, and a knowledge of the grants available from official sources.[4]

Direct and speedy contact with the parties who might become involved in bitter conflict is another objective of countryside management and, where the officer can secure acceptance or a compromise, short term agreements, subject to review at the end of the period, are sensible because of the rapid changes occurring in the social and economic situations, and the natural suspicion of anyone to be tied indefinitely to an agreement in which they are giving up something.

The Commission recommends that the officer should initially undertake small tasks which are unlikely to raise opposition, because this modest beginning will build up an atmosphere of trust. Examples of these initial tasks are given as 'clearing litter and small-scale dereliction; clearing, way-marking and surfacing footpaths; making small car parks or passing bays; repairing or putting in fencing and walling to counter trespassing and vandalism;

amenity planting and other landscape and wildlife conservation work.'[5] When trust has been established between the officer and the various parties concerned with the rural landscape, it may be possible to secure their participation in a management plan. Under current legislation in Britain, such a plan has no legal status, but if it is prepared by all concerned, it could be just as effective in the long run as a statutory plan prepared by one party. When the management plan affects only one landowner, and he is willing and even anxious to participate, a legally binding agreement is possible, as in the case of Upton Castle in Wales (see Chapter Three).

Support for conservation measures in the countryside with the emphasis on preservation often comes from commuters and weekenders who take up residence in the countryside because of the attractive environment which they hope will remain unchanged. The true countryman, depending upon the countryside for his livelihood, supports changes relevant to the prevailing social and economic conditions. While the commuter and the weekender may solve the problem of conserving the fabric of the villages, the true countryman may be forced by changing economic conditions to relinquish his task of maintaining the rural landscape if he is not allowed to sweep away anything which obstructs a conveyor belt landscape bringing him immediate and short-term profit. Thus, we are in a situation where the new residents of the countryside are ardent advocates of conservation, but have not been forthcoming in making up the incomes of farmers who may suffer financial loss by keeping to traditional methods.

Local authorities in Britain have some opportunities for, and duties relating to, conservation in the countryside, such as developing and managing country parks. At a more general level, the Planning Department of the Essex County Council has a policy placing some rural lanes under protective measures. The Norfolk County Council operate a massive countywide tree planting programme with the aid of Countryside Commission grants; a specific area is chosen each year, and every farmer and landowner within the area is asked to participate — more than two-thirds of those approached under this scheme have been willing to co-operate. Conservation of the rural landscape often involves areas some distance away from a site on which some development project is proposed in order that visual screening and wind shelter are preserved or required; this raises the question of carrying out works on someone else's land, because he does not want to sell and the owner of the development project does not want to buy. The participation of a local authority, as a financially disinterested party, can be helpful, and if concessions to the remote landowner were made if he agreed to the planting so that the land was exempted from death duties and other forms of taxation, what is called 'off site' planting might have a better chance of success.

Local authorities in Britain are the major bodies through which the reclamation of derelict landscape is effected because it is through them that the Central Government grant system works. Reclamation is, in essence, conservation — sometimes restoring the landscape to its basic state before the industry, which caused the dereliction, commenced operations. When the reclaimed landscape takes on a different form to the basic state (e.g. to give larger areas of better orientated gentle slopes), the objectives of conserva-

tion have to some extent been observed. Unless the original landscape was of considerable historical importance (and one can argue that some of the derelict landscapes of industry should be kept intact for their representation of a phase of history) or unique in its beauty, there is not a very strong case for exactitude in restoration when the proposal may be an improved landscape from both fertility and appearance points of view. The most difficult decision would occur when the landscape had been relatively infertile, open

5.4 *Cadman's Pond in the New Forest. An example of the conservation policy of the Forestry Commission's Committee for controlling access, car parking and recreation in the sensitive and much visited landscape of the New Forest. The Commission's interest in providing for recreation in its forests dates from the establishment of the first forest park in 1935, and the scale of the conservation problem is shown by the fact that about 24 million persons enjoy the forest amenities each year. (Courtesy of the Forestry Commission)*

5.5 *The felling programme in forests poses a continuous problem in the conservation of landscape. There has been criticism in the past over the unsympathetically shaped bare 'patches' in the felling of commercial forests, but careful planning of the areas to be felled, both in time and in relation to the topography and important viewing points, can produce satisfactory results. The bare 'patch' in this view of the Gwydr Forest in North Wales is sympathetically related to the landscape. (Courtesy of the Forestry Commission)*

moorland which to some people is not particularly distinguished compared with a well-treed valley landscape, but is much loved by other people. If the proposed reclamation includes a re-arranged topography and shelter belts to give better drainage, orientation and shelter, and an unfriendly substratum has been disturbed by the industry so that the new soil profile is better than that on the open moorland, the

first group of people and, no doubt, those concerned in agricultural production will be well pleased. For the second group, there will be concern at the change from the traditional landscape, but even that may have been changed from its natural state by sheep grazing or periodic burning.

Tree planting, in the many forms of hedgerow and boundary trees, small groups and plantations, woodlands and forests, is critical to the appearance and biological health of most rural areas, and has a significant role to play in providing shelter for fields

5.6 *The National Trust has a policy for conserving the parkland and woodland landscape at Petworth Park in West Sussex. But without such a policy over past generations, there will inevitably be gaps in the planting. In this illustration, the stumps of two felled trees can be seen, with three young trees planted as replacements. Meanwhile, three of the mature trees remain.*

and orchards. From the point of view of conservation, there is much to say about a country's tree population. Some woodlands and forests, and the occasional tree in which Royalty once hid from would-be captors, are historically notable. The New Forest in the South of England is the best known of the tree population remaining from historical times, although the reader will be familiar with examples in his own locality, like the Caledonian Forest in the Scottish Highlands and Sherwood Forest in Nottinghamshire. The New Forest is not only one of the few extant forests from the time when strict laws controlled hunting – and thus conserved the forest – but ancient management practices and customs survive there. Despite these ancient conservation measures, the invasion by visitors resulting from their increased mobility has produced pollution, erosion and wildlife problems too great for natural processes to keep in check, but positive conservation measures over six or seven years have just about

brought the New Forest back to a restored state which can be kept without deterioration. Conservationists must always be interested in the administrative arrangements which lead to successful results and, in the case of the New Forest, a Committee was set up to study the problems, consisting of members from the Forestry Commission, the County Council, the Nature Conservancy Council and the Verderers who are the long established custodians of the Forest. The Committee's recommendations were put into effect and included the reduction of 1200 access points

5.7 *This old engraving of an estate at Dunham Massie in Cheshire shows the appearance of the landscape soon after it was planted. The young trees have not grown to the extent when they will lose their regularity, but this inevitably happens in the course of time, making the felling of a tree here and there less of a visual impact. Nevertheless, the problem of tree replacement is difficult when the original plan did not provide for a continuous programme of renewal.*

Dunham Massie, the Seat of the Rt. Honble. George Earle of Warrington.
in the County Palatine of Chester, 1697.

where cars penetrated the Forest from the roads to 140 access points leading to car parks, and permanent and overflow camp sites (particularly at National Holiday weekends) limited to 5000 and 1500 pitches respectively. The New Forest policy proves that while conservation measures often mean some restriction of absolute freedom of the individual, they do in the long run preserve a sensible degree of freedom. The fact that several interested parties were invited on to the Committee added to the technical

5.8 *The foresters of the National Trust at work in the woodlands at Cragside, Rothbury in Northumberland. At this estate, many paths had become overgrown with the years, and views that were in the original concept of the estate landscape had been blocked by dense vegetation. There are also the normal tasks of keeping woodlands in a state of good health.*

knowhow and represents the public interest by preserving the beauty of the Forest whilst enabling it to be seen in a way that avoids damage.

The policy of the Forestry Commission in its numerous British forests to bar private cars from most forest roads is an example of both preserving the tranquillity of the forest environment and conserving the forest landscape by avoiding the necessity for road surfaces suitable for a high density of private cars. These surfaces are, of course, suitable for the Commission's own vehicles and for the walker where a forest is open for recreation. There are the problems of litter, and more seriously fire, which are not helped by the difficulty of surveillance in the limited vision within forests. Educating the public conscience, providing adequate wardening services and closing forests in high-risk periods are established preventitive

measures, supported by forest layouts with firebreaks.

Forests which rely upon their continued existence because of the timber produced can be managed in a way which accords with conservation principles by designing the layout in sympathy with the topography and arranging felling programmes which do not produce ugly 'holes' in the landscape. But in all the several ways in which trees grow or are planted as an important part of the landscape there is always the problem of age; sometimes a tree dies of old age and sometimes it will be felled when it has reached maturity so that replanting can take place to provide for the future. This is a conservation dilemma, concerned with appearance rather than with sound arboricultural practice, and illustrated by the lime tree avenues at Hampton Court, near London, which were planted in the 17th century; the Advisory Committee on Forestry in the Royal Parks advocates a policy of clear felling of the 180 limes encircling the Great Fountain Garden and replanting with young limes, so that precise symmetry and formality between one tree and another is maintained, although many years would have to pass before this effect made an impact. Contrary to this advice is local opposition to a barren appearance for some years, and advocacy for a policy of selective felling and replanting even if this means forgoing the precise symmetry and formality which will be only really effective in years to come. There are many considerations which make a decision on these conservation matters difficult: for many years when a landscape was first planted, the trees were small saplings or standards whose appearance had to be accepted and this was the appearance of the landscape to the first generation who planted it; many landscapes originally conceived to be as symmetrical and formal as a classical building have become softened by the trees developing slightly different forms, thus selective felling and planting is not regarded as too detrimental to the appearance which has lost its precise symmetry and formality; some day each tree will eventually die, but it is unlikely this will happen all at the same time, but future generations could accuse us of neglect if all the trees were in such a bad state that clear felling was essential and they have to accept many years of a newly planted landscape; aged trees may fall and cause damage, or even loss of life; and sometimes clear felling of some species before the trees have come the the end of their lives may bring in finance which would cover the cost of felling and replanting. These considerations

can be set one against the other, but it is essential that the final arbiter has advice from the best 'tree doctors' and from landscape experts, whilst each side involved in public debate on the future of the aged trees of avenues, groups or plantations will need to be prepared to support or debunk each consideration, as the case may be.

Many of the coppiced woodlands are of historical interest as well as contributing a particular appearance to landscape.[6] Considered as a forestry management technique, coppicing was practised in the Middle Ages, and there is every justification on historical grounds as well as visual to conserve some coppiced woodlands, although the market for the kind of timber they produce has declined. If, however, coppiced woodlands are to be conserved, frequent cutting over is necessary, and this is unlikely to take place unless a market can be found for the small diameter poles. The National Trust is faced with this problem, and while it is converting some of its coppiced woodlands to high forest, it is keeping small areas under the old system, realizing that coppiced woods are important local constituents of landscape. Various forms of wildlife find that coppiced woodland habitats are very suitable for their food and shelter requirements – a fact which gives another reason for their conservation.

The general directive in the Countryside Act 1968 (see also Section 66 of the Countryside Act, 1967), requiring public bodies to have regard to the desirability of conserving the natural beauty and amenity of the countryside of England and Wales, has provided the opportunity to challenge at public inquiries any proposals made by these bodies which act against conservation, but it is a weakness of the Act that public bodies are not required to account for the ways in which they are carrying out conservation measures, and there is no provision for enforcement. There are also similar directives in the Scottish legislation.

However, the Ministry of Agriculture, Fisheries and
Overleaf

5.9 *A typical example of a coppiced woodland, in this case planted with sweet chestnut trees. These woodlands are usually connected with some other economic activity, such as the production of poles for hop fields, and many of them will be of historical value as new techniques develop in the associated economic activity. Coppices also have a particular character as elements of landscape, but they can only be kept as coppices with regular cutting. (Courtesy of the Forestry Commission)*

Food's policy is to have regard to this obligation, both when giving advice generally to farmers on proposals for improvements and when considering applications for grant under its capital grant schemes. The Ministry bears the countryside interest in mind throughout its work and its officials keep closely in touch with the Department of the Environment, the Countryside Commission, the National Park authorities, the Nature Conservancy Council, local planning authorities and other bodies at all appropriate levels. The Agricultural Development and Advisory Service co-operates in projects and experiments and seeks by publicity and advice to promote the concepts of conservation and landscape appreciation. These concepts are specifically considered before grant aid is approved on farm investments.

The scheduling of areas as National Parks, Areas of Outstanding Natural Beauty, Conservation Areas, Country Parks, Green Belts, Nature Reserves and Sites of Special Scientific Interest has made a big contribution to the safeguarding of landscape in Britain, especially because some funds are available for conserving the landscape of these areas. Persons and organizations committed to conservation should try and persuade the Central Government to place areas of special quality, and which are at risk, under the protection of one of these categories. Planning authorities can themselves act directly to safeguard landscape through their responsibilities for granting approval to applications for a development or change of use proposal, and it is always possible to make representations to them, if only informally, about the conservation aspects of an application. Planning authorities have the authority to make Tree Preservation Orders and should be ready to listen to a representation made to them; they can also take protective action when, as the law requires, they must be given adequate notice of a proposal to fell a tree in a Conservation Area.[7] Whether acting for or against a proposal to fell a tree, any person concerned should weigh up pros and cons which are similar to those suggested for considering the fate of the old trees of an historic landscape (see page 55).

The many different kinds of area in the countryside which can be scheduled in Britain for protection are evidence of the concern people have for the rural landscape, now subject to so many pressures for change. The Countryside Commission has suggested yet another kind of area for scheduling – Areas of Mainly Open Country and which lie within National Parks; this

suggestion is likely to meet opposition because these areas are currently attractive for afforestation and can respond to soil improvement techniques. As with most provisions now relating to what can or cannot happen to the land, and thus the landscape, changes are made from time to time, and the effectiveness of the Areas of Outstanding Natural Beauty as a means of conserving and improving the landscape is currently being examined under the aegis of the Countryside Commission; giving evidence or making representations to official bodies who are conducting an inquiry is one means whereby advocates of conservation can influence policy.

The launching of the operation 'Enterprise Neptune' by the National Trust in 1965 was an example of a positive conservation measure, and the money raised by the campaign enabled 622 kilometres (387 miles) of coastline in England and Wales to benefit from the Trust's protection. In Scotland 127 kilometres (79 miles) and in Northern Ireland 56 kilometres (35 miles) of coastline have similarly been acquired. Protecting the coastline from erosion can be aided by central government grants under the Coast Protection Act, 1949.

Some of the scheduled areas of landscape have to be protected from access by the general public, but with most of them, the expenditure of public funds justifies the conservation of footpaths, bridleways and lanes which make access possible and enable the landscape to be traversed. These means of access are themselves landscape features and justify conservation techniques which retain their beauty, instead of merely repairing the walking surface. In general, the responsibility for keeping the footpaths in order rests with the county councils as highway authorities, but there is also the matter of the preservation of footpaths which are in danger of disappearing; the Ramblers' Association has estimated that over 1200 Orders are made for footpath closures and diversions in England and Wales each year. This probably means that around 800 kilometres (500 miles) of paths are affected in this way each year. The walker is not served as well as the motorist regarding the upkeep of the routes he traverses, but he is more concerned that footpaths remain open than wanting a perfect macadam surface; indeed, footpaths in the countryside lie well within the scope of voluntary labour as regards maintenance.

Landscape conservation has been extended considerably in recent years by voluntary work, with the restoration of some canals gaining most publicity and adding to the mileage available for pleasure cruising. In common with other public bodies, the British Waterways Board, which manages the greater part of the canal system in Britain, has a statutory duty towards conservation. The Board, however, is limited in the restoration work by the available funds from a quiet transportation system which, if fully used, would relieve pressures on other noisy transportation systems – in particular reducing environmental loss from the excessive use of the roads and thus contributing to the conservation of the peace of the countryside. The basic conservation task with the canals is the maintenance of the sides and bottom of the water channel and, under the Transport Act 1968,

the British Waterways Board is only required to maintain the towpaths where they are required for access for repairs and are the only means of access to a recreational facility; yet, the towpaths are a recreational asset in themselves and an essential part of the canal landscape. The legalities of towpaths are somewhat involved and the responsibility for their conservation is rarely placed upon any body which is compelled to look after them. With the diminished

5.10 *A group of members of the Ramblers' Association of Heathfield in East Sussex at work on footpath clearance. This is an example of the good work carried out in landscape conservation by many volunteer groups, and was aided by some members attending a weekend school on footpath clearance. (Courtesy of the Ramblers' Association)*

5.11 *Volunteer work in conservation is perhaps best known in connection with canal restoration. Here, around 1000 volunteers cleared rubbish from the Ashton Canal at Dukinfield Junction, Manchester, over one weekend, saving an estimated £20,000. This canal became derelict in 1961, but was reopened to boats in 1974. Little comment is needed on the fine architecture of the bridge and, indeed, most examples of canal architecture are well related to the landscape, and merit preservation. (Courtesy of Hugh McKnight)*

attraction of the roads as a means of travel by pedestrians and cyclists through the countryside, the canal towpaths, if brought within a definite maintenance responsibility as in the case of the roads, would go some way towards compensating this considerable interest among those who do pay taxes and rates.[8]

There are many examples now in Britain of the work volunteers have carried out in canal restoration on the initiative of the Inland Waterways Association and the Waterways Recovery Group, and further work has been undertaken through the Job Creation Programme, such as Rochdale's employment of nearly 140 young people for cleaning up its canals and their surroundings. The Job Creation Programme and its replacement by job opportunities through the Manpower Services Commission were set up to provide employment during a time of economic difficulty in the 1970's. The British Trust for Conservation Volunteers has an excellent record of achievement in practical conservation and in giving advice to groups who established themselves for particular projects. The scope of the conservation work on which the Trust can give technical and organizational help is very wide as indicated by maintaining and replanting hedgerows, repairing stone walls, clearing ponds and streams, protective works for wildlife, and scrub clearance.[9] Voluntary work does encounter some problems, such as insurance cover, training in construction techniques, access to derelict and damaged areas, and competition with paid labour, although usually the work would not, in fact, ever be carried out by paid labour. Another benefit to conservation is that the involvement of people on a voluntary basis can only add to their interest in the landscape. Most local authorities will give moral, if not financial support, to properly organized and supervised voluntary work for conservation, and can often give valuable technical advice in an unofficial capacity.

Conservation in the countryside entails a watchful eye on the vast area of land, and much of it is difficult to reach. The limited resources of those official bodies and voluntary organizations, whose objective among many is to look out for anti-conservation proposals and operations, can be supplemented by mobilizing young people in schools to report the tipping of waste, litter, pollution, erosion, damage to structures and vegetational decline. But if this reporting is not followed up by remedial action, the interest of schools will surely decline. This observing and reporting can be given educational value and develop a sense of responsibility for the environment.

The planning authorities have great responsibilities for the conservation of landscape, though, as explained earlier, their influence in Britain is limited over agricultural and afforestation lands. They can approve or disapprove proposals for development which are not exempt from the planning process and which often constitute a material change to the landscape. In giving approval, planning authorities can impose conditions on the way the change takes place; for example, opencast mining may have to conform to safeguards against excessive noise and traffic in nearby villages, or, in giving approval to the impounding of a reservoir in an area of fine landscape, planting and grading works may be required which, in the course of time, will help to produce a different, but also fine, landscape. Whether the procedures for giving advice to farmers on conservation (and taking this into account in approving grant aid) by the Ministry of Agriculture, Fisheries and Food (see page 58) could be strengthened if landscape conditions, such as some planning authorities impose, were made a formal condition of a grant for purposes like land drainage and marginal land improvement, is open to question because the more gentle approach often yields better results with the countryman than the impersonal legal restraint. The same procedure could well apply to forestry proposals with the landscape expertise now available in the Forestry Commission extended to review private afforestation proposals. If any extra cost was involved over the normal application for grant aid because of the landscape conditions, the developer's objection would, in all probability, fail if the grant took account of this, and everyone would benefit by the resulting good landscape although at some extra cost to the nation.

The registration of common land in England goes some way to protecting these quite considerable areas from development, many of them with historical interest and good landscape quality, but the

Overleaf
5.12 *An example of a Demonstration Farm plan under the Countryside Commission's project to set up a number of Demonstration Farms in different parts of the country. In this example of the Tynllan Demonstration Farm, the areas shown by different textures were the results of acceptability, compromise and rejection where a proposal would conflict with the commercial farming interests. (Courtesy of Clouston, Cobham and Partners, and Messrs N. Davies and E. E. Bebb of the farm in question)*

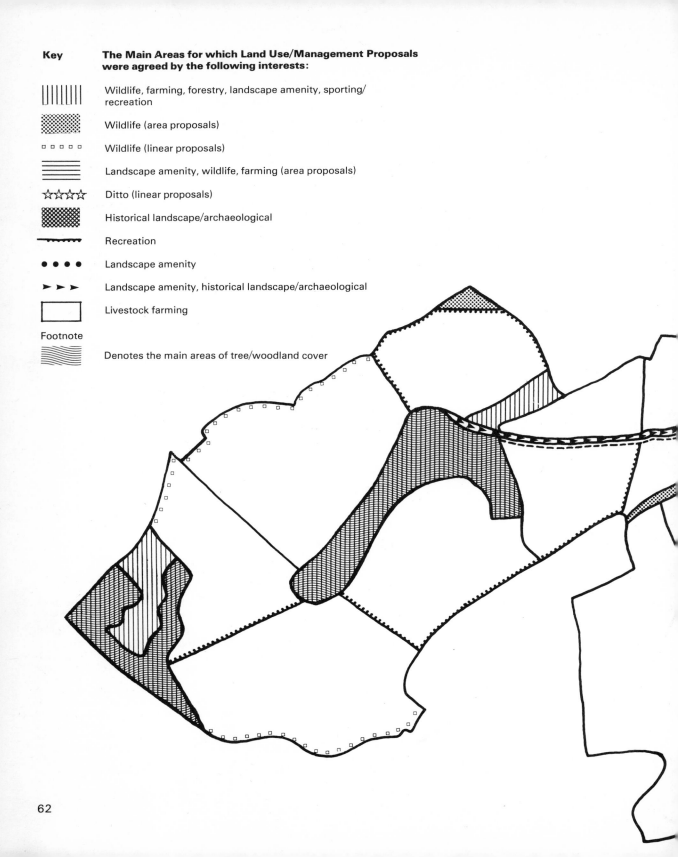

Key

The Main Areas for which Land Use/Management Proposals were agreed by the following interests:

|||||||| Wildlife, farming, forestry, landscape amenity, sporting/recreation

░░░░ Wildlife (area proposals)

▫ ▫ ▫ ▫ ▫ Wildlife (linear proposals)

≡≡≡ Landscape amenity, wildlife, farming (area proposals)

☆☆☆☆ Ditto (linear proposals)

▨▨▨ Historical landscape/archaeological

▬᭡᭡᭡᭡᭡ Recreation

● ● ● ● Landscape amenity

► ► ► Landscape amenity, historical landscape/archaeological

▭ Livestock farming

Footnote

〰〰〰 Denotes the main areas of tree/woodland cover

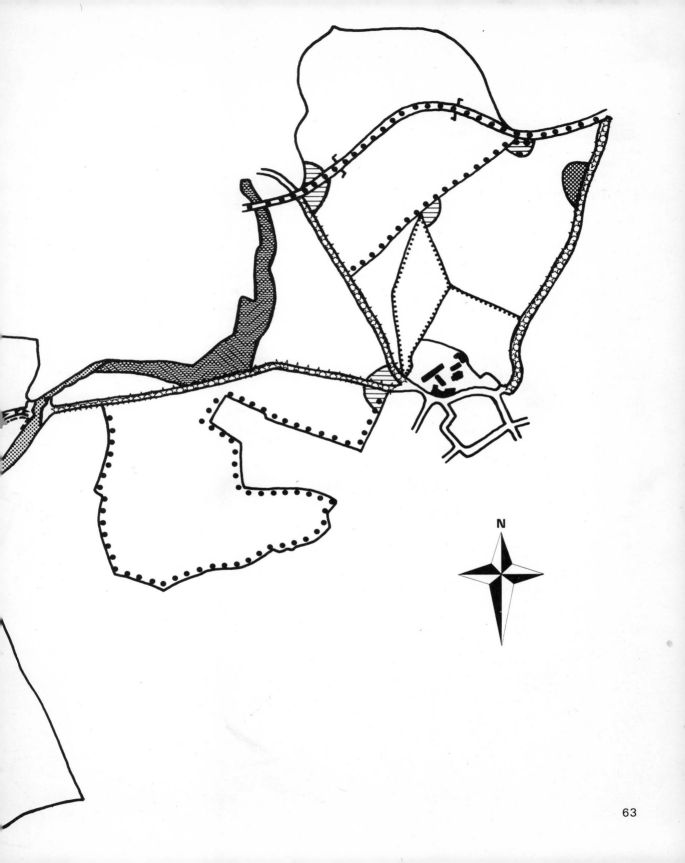

N

immediate problem is one of the time taken to identify and research all the contenders for the title of common land (see Chapter Ten).

Conservation by example is a policy which can be more successful than conservation by enforcement, and is likely to be a more acceptable way of achieving the desired result in democratic countries than by the latter method. The Countryside Commission's experiment to collaborate with some farmers in setting up a number of demonstration farms will, it is hoped, show that conservation and modern agriculture can be compatible; if the experiment produces the desired result, its influence should be considerable because the proof will come from the farmers themselves who are involved in the project, and not from some remote research station. When two apparently conflicting objectives regarding the cultivated landscape are present, and neither side is able to dominate the issue, a compromise solution is the only hope if the landscape is not eventually to return to a wild state because the farmer or forester would give up in the face of competition from their fellows who were able to introduce modern methods. Three examples which are compromise solutions will illustrate the point. The future of the Broads landscape in East Anglia is in doubt because of the increase in its recreational use by boats and there is always the question whether its 'artificial' character resulting from drainage and other works can remain without some form of management; the Countryside Commission put forward four possible courses of action and a short term expedient and, as a result of the response to these proposals, has accepted a compromise solution of a consortium of local authorities and interested bodies which has a two-year period in which to prove that it can respond effectively to the conservation challenge. The second example is the suggestion made to the Hedgerow and Farm Timber Committee under the aegis of the Forestry Commission that the removal of hedgerows should be compensated by planting tree belts around farm boundaries, thus allowing the farmer ample scope and flexibility with his use of the land, while maintaining a tree population in the countryside;[10] this suggestion may have some impact now with the present increasing interest in the tree population of the countryside which has lost so very many trees with the removal of hedgerows and as a result of Dutch elm disease. The third example is the reduction in the area of permanent grassland in some 18th-century parklands by turning some parts, usually remote from the house, over to ley cultivation, whilst retaining the woodland, tree belt and tree group structure of the landscape.

The demonstration farm experiment and the suggestion for tree belts around farm boundaries are examples of selective conservation combined with profitable land management. Nevertheless, the heavy taxation endured by farmers and landowners encourages monocultural practices and more and more mechanization which can act contrary to conservation principles unless carefully monitored.

[1] UNESCO, *Recommendation concerning the safeguarding of the beauty and character of landscapes and sites* (Paris, 1962).

[2] Westmacott, R., and Worthington, T., *New Agricultural Landscapes* (HMSO, 1974)

[3] *Agriculture and the Countryside (Strutt Report)* (HMSO, 1978).

[4] R. J. S. Hookway, *'Countryside Management, the development of techniques'*, Town and Country Planning Summer School papers (London, 1977).

[5] *Ibid.*

[6] The practice of coppicing occurs when the growth of new shoots from tree stumps of suitable species are periodically cut to produce straight and small-diameter poles.

[7] See Chapter Ten.

[8] For an informative review of towpaths, including their legal status, see M. F. Tanner, *The Potential of Towpaths as Waterside Footpaths* (Water Space Amenity Commission; London, 1977).

[9] A. Brooks, *Hedging* (British Trust for Conservation Volunteers: London, 1975). *Waterways and Wetlands* (*ibid.*, 1976). *Dry Stone Walling* (*ibid.*, 1977).

[10] This suggestion was given in evidence by the author to the Hedgerow and Farm Committee in 1955.

Chapter 6

Conservation for amenity

In a materialistic world it is fortunate that there is sufficient interest and concern to canvass and work for keeping alive those landscapes which were developed mainly to give relaxation and visual pleasure. Today, many of these landscapes are accessible to the public at large; with their beauty, their quietude, or as a medium for active recreation, they continue to give pleasure and relief from the noisy concrete jungle in which most of us have to live. But the circumstances in which they originally existed have changed; taxation and inflation have reduced the money that the inheritors of these landscapes can afford to spend on their maintenance, and the labour costs of the dwindling army of gardeners and foresters cause an owner to consider how he can simplify the maintenance tasks of gardens and estate landscapes. When these landscapes have important historic and cultural associations, it is even more important to try and find some way of conserving them.

Ownership in whatever form is the basis of action for conserving gardens, parkland and woodlands; while this remained within one family, and taxation and inflation were virtually unknown, upkeep was not a difficult problem. Now increased mobility and a wider interest in the beauties of landscape have brought these amenity landscapes closer to everyone, with the result that there is a large number of potential visitors who would need special arrangements and additional maintenance work on the landscape if they are to be given access. With these problems and the wider interest, the sole owner of an estate has to consider what changes he can make if he agrees to allow public access to his estate. Vesting the estate in some form of trust helps with the taxation and death duties problem. Handing over the estate to some national

Trust today usually means that the estate must have enough income, with tax exemption, to cover safeguarding and maintenance by a Trust, although in compensation some form of continuous residence can sometimes be arranged for the donor. There are also some examples where an estate has been taken over as a Country Park by the local authority.

Some owners have the energy and initiative to introduce a commercial element into their estates by charging admission but unless enterprises like wildlife parks and restaurants are established, admission charges alone rarely contribute more than the absolute minimum needed to avoid deterioration. Joint interest in an estate, so that the burdens are shared, is another possibility, as at Cragside in Northumberland where the National Trust and the County Council have accepted responsibility – for the house with the former and the Country Park aspect with the latter. At Culzean Country Park in Scotland, there is another example of collaboration between the National Trust for Scotland and a group of local authorities. The Management Agreement at Upton

Overleaf

6.1 *Cragside, near Rothbury in Northumberland, is a recently opened National Trust property set in a romantic upland landscape planted mainly with conifers, and invaded by rhododendrons. The Trust accepted responsibility for the house, and the County Council has taken over the extensive grounds as a Country Park – an example of sensible collaboration in the conservation of landscape and its associated buildings. Work is now in hand, not only to carry out essential repairs to the house, but also to open up views which have been lost through the growth of vegetation. Here, one of the best views of the house has been opened up.*

Castle in Wales is also an example of joint interest though of a different kind (see Chapter Three).

When one of these joint agreements is entered into, each party will require safeguards to protect its own special interests, and the following are typical of what may be required:

1. Public access, but with restrictions on certain areas and routes, and on the use of vehicles.

2. Avoidance of damage to, or interference with, the landscape including wildlife; for example, access by dogs allowed only if on a leash.

3. Restrictions on shooting, fishing and bathing.

4. Behaviour – disorderley conduct, fire risk, depositing litter, noise, hindering persons in authority.

5. Limitation on the number and size of eating facilities.

6. Adequate provision of car parks, toilets, and litter baskets and collection.

Where the agreement covers the right of access by the public, the legality aspect can be negated by a provision that the right of access does not apply to anyone defaulting over the safeguards. It is very likely that a joint agreement would include the completion of some repair and improvement works, and a management plan of a more detailed kind than suggested for rural landscapes (see Chapter Five), and which included regular maintenance, should be part of the agreement.

When an amenity landscape is made accessible to the general public, it is only right that they should contribute to its conservation either through taxation or rates to the national or local government and then back to those responsible for its maintenance in the form of a regular grant. There is an argument which

6.2 *A view along the circuit road which makes a one-way traffic system possible at Cragside (see Fig. 6.1). The maintenance programme includes cutting back the invasive rhododendrons and other shrubs in order that vehicles and pedestrians may pass unimpeded. Ideally, planting alongside roads should be designed to avoid this frequent maintenance.*

says that it is unfair that everyone should contribute in this way, whilst only a percentage of the population is likely to visit these landscapes; but the same argument can be levelled against any form of art or leisure activity supported in similar ways, and at the cost of policing gatherings attended by a small percentage of the population. Clearly if regular grants are not available, the visiting public must expect to contribute

6.3 *The house at The Shadows estate in New Iberia, Louisiana, USA. The conservation plan involved disposing of several thousand acres and leaving only 3 acres immediately around the house. Because the scale of the landscape was now so different, the 3 acres were developed as a densely enclosed garden, arranged to give shade in a region with a hot climate. This is an example where conservation has to accept change to prevent complete obliteration.*

through admission charges or by commercial development in keeping with the public's recreational interests. With the latter method, there is a limit to the number of estates which will attract a sufficient number of visitors to produce the necessary income for upkeep – planning authorities may yet have to take into account this possibility of flooding the market if too many applications for the commercial development of estates with landscape quality come into their offices, although they would be hard put to refuse any application which might save a fine landscape from deterioration. When an amenity landscape is taken over to become a Country Park, there is legislation which enables public funds to be used for the conservation of the landscape, but it would be a pity if this meant giving up the farming and forestry operations

6.4 *The Cragside estate (see Fig. 6.1) is again used as an example of landscape conservation. Here, a planned view in the original concept had become overgrown until the recent new management adopted a policy of bringing back some of the original views by clearing away invasive vegetation.*

which have been the reason behind the appearance of many of the parklands and woodlands of amenity landscapes. In fact, it may be possible for their upkeep to be largely financed from these operations, perhaps by linking them with adjoining farms.

Most of the historic amenity landscapes were designed to be used only by the owner, his family and his guests, although it will be recalled that the formal gardens in the French manner on the Continent had wide paths for accommodating the crowds associated with Court life (see p. 33). Some modification of the original design may be necessary to cater for today's public with its wider interest and increased mobility, if wear and tear or damage to the landscape are not to occur. A few paths may have to be widened and others closed off, and their surfaces renewed with a stronger material. All these changes to historic landscapes require a sensitive design approach which understands the stylistic characteristics, and nothing which is not absolutely essential should be undertaken.

Several references have been made to management plans, and one cannot repeat too often that the conservation of a landscape requires a plan and description of work in the same way that the original grading and construction and planting were based on similar documents. Conservation plans are usually drawn up in a manner which indicates the phases of a programme for restoration and the seasonal maintenance operations or management aspects. The plans should be based on two considerations: first, the date to which restoration works should revert if restoration is necessary (see Chapter Two); and second, ensuring that deterioration and changes do not happen once restoration has taken place, such as a lake gradually overtaken by reed growth, or clear felling a planted woodland of one species and failing to replant so that natural regeneration of many species does not take place.

The first decision to make in preparing a conservation plan is the extent of the area included in it. Reducing the size of an estate through the sale of some of the land to produce additional income, or reducing the size of the area to be conserved so that the rest can be given over to an income-producing use, are always matters for regret, but this may be the only way of conserving the most important part from the historical or appearance points of view if no other way of overcoming financial problems is available. An extreme example of this always regrettable necessity was The Shadows estate in New Iberia, Louisiana, USA, where an estate of several thousand acres was reduced to a mere three acres of landscape which was changed to enclose the house and its garden from the development taking place on the land released. In such an example, the decision on the minimum amount of land which must be retained requires careful study – whether reducing the area of a parkland landscape makes a nonsense of it, or whether the remaining area of this kind of landscape can be modified to produce the smaller scale appropriate to the reduced area without losing the historical significance. At The Shadows estate the house is preserved, but the landscape of its three acres has been changed to an intimate garden from what was a typical large estate landscape. If an estate, which has be be reduced in size, had a garden landscape immediately around the house, the problem is more easily resolved, though it is always regrettable to be forced to change an original concept if it has historical or visual significance.

When there has to be a major reduction in the size of an estate and there is no definite central feature which would make a smaller and different landscape seem logical, the following questions could well be asked:

1. Does the estate have examples of several different styles of landscape or historical periods? If so, retaining a small area of each is important, and the plan of sale and development of the land taken should incorporate the linking of these small areas by 'landscape strips'.

2. Can the framework, such as the tree belts and groups, be retained by allowing only low density dispersed development, such as detached houses spread about an historical parkland in a way that linked them with the tree belts and groups, and with a leasehold or freehold arrangement which restricts conventional gardening operations?

3. Is the landscape of a kind where previous owners have modified the original layout from time to time? If so, the case against a further modification is weakened, unless a complete change of use, say from woodland to high density housing, is planned.

Landscape responds to the life lived in it, with the result that there is always the problem of how and whether landscape change can be prevented if one wishes to avoid the museum type of landscape. A test of this situation is to ask whether a replacement or modification will be better than the landscape as it now exists, and this often became at maturity rather different from the way the designer and his client may have conceived it. This is evident in the aerial views in many 17th- and 18th-century engravings of landscapes which depicted the trees at about one quarter of the way to maturity. Thus, views across the landscape, which may have been planned by the designer, may have become obscured as a result of adventitious plants as well as the growth of the original planted vegetation. Some clearance of vegetation in an historical landscape may be closer to historical accuracy than a policy of preserving everything. It could be argued that, in order to bring some historical

landscapes back to the designer's concept, all the planting would have to be removed and replanting carried out in order that the trees are at a youthful stage of growth.

It is not unusual to find that the details of an historic landscape have been changed through the years, but if the objective is to restore to the appearance at a particular date, a reasonable assumption can be made about it by consulting contemporary books which illustrate elements like parterres and garden artefacts; also, other gardens in a good state of preservation can be accepted as examples. There is latitude with the selection of plant species because owners of gardens often changed them from time to

6.5 *The point is well made about finding sites for car parks in a landscape conservation plan in this illustration of a new car park at Cragside in Northumberland, where the National Trust has selected a site which makes the most of the screening effect of the topography and the existing vegetation.*

time, but it is appropriate to select from the range of species in vogue at the historical date, and this information can be gathered from contemporary descriptions, lists, letters ordering plants and other similar sources. In any case, some varieties of plant species originally grown are no longer available, thus the aim should be to provide an appearance from the planting which is typical of the period. At Pitmeddan in Aberdeenshire, the National Trust for Scotland has created the patterning of the parterres from old records.

A conservation plan which makes provision for some public use of the landscape will require consideration of the access points and possibly closing some roads in the estate while improving others so that vehicles may be kept away from certain places to conserve the peace of the landscape. As part of the traffic arrangements, car parks are inevitable, their location being determined by the need to find areas which are screened or capable of being screened without difficulty, and also by the public approach roads outside the estate. Facilities like lavatories, picnic places and some provision for obtaining food when the number of visitors is likely to justify this as a commercial proposition should be provided. The footpaths will also probably need some modification and additions to direct people away from easily damaged areas, and to make some areas more accessible. All these facilities need to be noted in an information system, such as a leaflet guide, maps on boards at useful places showing the position reached and how to proceed, and notices at the various facilities. Notices should be visible, but sympathetically designed in relation to the landscape, although it is something of a problem to carry this out in an estate where different historical styles exist because information is best given in a consistent manner.

Day to day and seasonal maintenance under present conditions of labour, compared with those prevailing when the landscape was laid out, have to be taken into account in the conservation plan, and may require some simplification of the planting, but mechanical equipment if sympathetically used, watering points and sprinklers can simplify main-

tenance without altering very much of the original design. When there is no alternative except to simplify the details of the layout, it is important to keep the framework of the layout and to keep a record of any planting and construction work removed because these two objectives would allow the original appearance to be reinstated without difficulty, if circumstances make this possible. Examples of simplifying the planting are substituting long-life perennials in the patterning of a parterre to replace short-lived annuals and biennials, also grassing an area designed for herbaceous plants.

When a landscape is opened to the public, the fire risk increases, especially in woodlands and rough grass areas, and the conservation plan should include provisions to minimize the risk and for assisting the task of fire fighting. There is, however, the fact that a fire has a better chance of being spotted quickly if there are a lot of people moving about a landscape. It will not always be possible to expect that a water main of sufficient pressure exists and can be extended through the estate at a cost that the owner is likely to be able to meet. Introducing several small ponds is a possibility, but will depend upon the run off of rainwater from the topography and whether the ponds can be located without affecting the character of the landscape. Access to these ponds by fire fighting equipment is essential, and the Forestry Commission provision of local fire fighting points at the 'first aid' level could well be followed.

The conservation plan for a landscape open to the public should state the periods and times of day because these relate to the ability of the landscape to withstand wear and tear, and to recover from periods of intensive use. Alternatively, certain parts of the landscape might be closed for short periods or even on specified days. Also, the proposals for opening have to take into account the cost of additional staff, especially when certain days in the week, or times in the year, may bring in too small an income to be covered by the profitable days. A study is currently being carried out by Lady Minto's Scotland's Garden Scheme into the cost implications of managing gardens open to the public, which should produce useful information.

Chapter 7

Green and built landscapes in towns

When reference is made to 'urban landscape' today, the understanding which has become accepted over the last thirty years or so is the whole fabric of a town or village, where streets and buildings are more in evidence than the 'green landscape' of grass and trees. In the urban landscape the conservation of individual buildings and groups of architectural or historic interest is provided by legislation and financial aid in many countries, and there is now much information available on the principles and techniques which come within the scope of the architect.[1] Our concern, however, is with the conservation of the views or the town and village scene, and of parks, gardens, street planting and other examples of green landscape for which legislation and finance is available, but in a less direct form than for buildings; but the objectives of conserving both the built and the green landscapes, which are constituents of the urban landscape, are the same.

Landscape is often thought about as the appearance of a scene which can be viewed, although this is only one aspect among all those involved in the way it functions as living landscape. Nevertheless, in towns and villages planning controls which aim to preserve, enhance, or open up beautiful views, and hide ugly views, are perhaps the first objective when planning authorities or conservation groups are considering what proposals or safeguards should be included in a town or village plan. In order to achieve this objective, the compulsory purchase of land or controls on the exact position, form and height of buildings are likely to be necessary in order to achieve the conservation objectives of a plan when applications to develop are submitted. If proper provision for this objective is

made soon enough, development is not inhibited because when it comes to the point there are always other places to which it can go in a comprehensive planning scheme. The views of the City of London are one of many examples where the urban landscape, so well depicted by Canaletto and remaining more or less constant until the second half of this century, has lost its unique skyline of domes, towers and spires – the failure of a nation to conserve one of its best achievements by a far more sensitive control of the position, height and silhouette of new buildings than is now seen across the City.

The opening-up of views is not always the right policy because some buildings, like the smaller churches and houses of towns in the Middle Ages, are only seen in their correct environment when surrounded by other buildings. But historical accuracy may not deter people from admiring the new view produced by the clearance of the buildings around a particular building, especially when it can then be given a green landscape setting. The argument made previously that changes may have taken place several times to an admired landscape, and what is wrong with yet another change if well designed, is also put forward, leaving the decision makers with a difficult problem to resolve between amenity, of which we have two opinions, and historical accuracy.

Too often, the background to a view of some building is neglected in the planning provisions made to conserve the building and its immediate surroundings. The reasons for this neglect are the immensity of the task of extending conservation into the far distance, and the fact that the background often extends as a circle around the building as the observer moves

7.1 *The ruins of the outer areas of the Castle at Newcastle upon Tyne overlook the River Tyne. The City recently carried out a conservation scheme on the ruins which included repairs to the stonework, arranging access to the different levels down the river bank, and providing planting. The result has been that a sensible use for the ruins, requiring only sensitive modifications, has not only brought a derelict area back to life, but preserved an important element in the City's history. (Courtesy of the City of Newcastle upon Tyne Planning Department)*

about. A major step towards this kind of conservation is the control of the height of new building and of new tree planting throughout an area of urban landscape where expansive and distant views are important. Some planning authorities have taken the trouble to fly balloons to the height of a proposed development in order to assess the visual implications of a proposal. Another device for assessing the effect of new proposals upon the urban landscape was in operation

for Stockholm's central area, and comprised a model of the streets and buildings, with each building removable in order that a model of a proposed building could be substituted and its visual effect assessed.

The preservation of a building needs consideration from two different points of view. It can be judged on architectural and historical grounds, including rarity and aesthetic appeal, but it can also occupy a key position in the appearance of an urban landscape even though the case for its preservation on the former grounds is not strong and as a result there may be very little to swing the decision one way or the other to preserve or to erect a new building which is

7.2 *The earthworks fortification of Frederikstad in Norway are used as a recreational walk around the town. Scheduling stone or earthworks ramparts as open space is one step towards their preservation, while in addition to their recreational value, they are important elements in the urban landscape.*

sympathetically designed. Here, as we are considering urban landscape, and not the individual building, some principles concerning the preservation of buildings in their role as elements of the urban landscape will not be out of place. Buildings, whose loss would destroy the continuity of a street scene which depended upon the harmonious relationship between all the buildings, merit preservation, as also those which help to frame a

7.3 *A typical Garden City view at Welwyn, where the vegetation dominates the urban landscape. The Garden Cities have now passed into the history of town planning and, as such, apart from their environmental value, rank worthy of conservation. A problem that can arise is that trees planted too close to buildings inevitably lead to a demand from the residents to reduce the size of the trees and, unless this is done with sympathetic skill, the visual result can be disastrous.*

beautiful and interesting view, or hide an unpleasant view. The removal of a building and the substitution of a very different one can upset the scale of the scene by demoting a public building which was always, and should remain, the centre of visual attraction.

It has become fashionable to talk about 'planned ruins' where there is no prospect of saving a building as a functioning unit, and some essential works are carried out which will prevent further damage and ensure safety. But ruins, which have become ruins by neglect or disuse, can be adapted to serve a useful purpose; for example, the sitting areas overlooking the river in Newcastle upon Tyne which are the result of a sensitive design retaining the visual quality of the ruins while arranging sheltered places with views of the river and its banks.

An expensive project, though effective as a con-

servation measure of the urban landscape, is the retention of the façade of a building while constructing a new building behind. The purist may frown at this device, but it hardly amounts to deception because the original façade is still functional, forming one of the protective walls, and its doors and windows give access and light to the interior; in any case, many of the interiors of buildings whose façades are important in the urban landscape have been changed several times in one way or another. The fear of many people is that there is little confidence that the problem of designing new façades to fit into an urban landscape of quality has been solved at the present time except in a few cases.

A common feature of historical cities in many parts of the world is the remains of a fortification system, and these are important elements of the urban landscape. There are generally two kinds of fortification which have survived – the stone wall (York and Canterbury) and the earthwork ramparts (e.g. Berwick upon Tweed). In addition to their historical significance, the visual contribution is more than that of a linear element because they often form a visual barrier between two different kinds of urban landscape, and they are a constant reminder that the city has an historical core which needs conserving. The recreational value of a route along the fortifications through urban fabric on both sides and which is unimpeded by vehicular traffic is an asset to a city, and

7.4 *In this view of the opened-up churchyard at the Parish Church of Darlington, Co. Durham, the best of the monuments have been incorporated into the design. The conservation of churchyards is a constant source of argument because very few of them have the appearance now associated with the date of the church, yet familiarity and sentiment resist proposals to bring them back closer to their original more open appearance. (Landscape architects: B. Hackett and B. Robson)*

7.5 *The terminus of the Erewash Canal at the Great Northern Basin, Langley Hill. This area was rescued from dereliction by volunteers, and was fully restored with a lock and swing bridge in 1973. The canal environment in towns often forms a very suitable place for residential and associated development. (Courtesy of Hugh McKnight)*

an extra advantage is the panoramic views obtained along the walk. In the past, the sites of fortification systems have sometimes been used as recreational open space, or as a ring road like the Ringstrasse in Vienna. In the latter example, while the fortifications have been demolished, the preservation of a continuous unbuilt-on area retains a linear element in the urban landscape, and is an example of conserving the idea without necessarily retaining the element.

Some urban landscapes, although 'built landcapes' in the sense they have streets and buildings, are dominated as regards their appearance by vegetation, and they have some difficult conservation problems. In the suburbs of many towns, and particularly industrial towns, the typical form taken by their growth in the 19th century was a number of large houses in their own grounds, densely planted with trees and shrubs which screened the houses from the road and from their neighbours when the vegetation developed beyond the initial planting stage. The changed domestic and economic situation today has left this kind of urban landscape at risk because the houses and grounds are too big as domestic accommodation and often too difficult to convert into several convenient units, resulting in demolition and dividing the land into sites for several small houses. Consequently, many trees and shrubs of great importance to the landscape are removed to make way for the new development. If the original building is taken over for a commercial use, a car park is sure to be constructed, and as time passes extensions are built, both meaning the loss of trees and shrubs. All is not lost, however, if greater care is taken in siting and planning the form of the buildings so that tree felling and shrub removal are minimized. Tree Preservation Orders, under British planning legislation, are one of the safeguards for the conservation of this kind of urban landscape.

The Garden City landscape is another example where the trees and shrubs are often more prominent than the paving of the streets and the buildings, but the vegetation has a more regular appearance than in the 19th century suburb because of the smaller plots which restricted the planting to limited areas in the same position in each plot and because of the more frequent use of avenue type planting along the roads. Up to the present time, this landscape is not so much at risk as in the 19th-century suburb, but some areas have a problem with the gardens being too large for many householders without some gardening help which is difficult to find and expensive to employ. With this kind of urban landscape, some of the trees, having grown close to maturity, take away light from the houses and as a result some of the owners arrange for removing the trees or for heavy pruning. Probably the trees were planted too closely to the buildings to allow them to grow naturally without interfering with daylight reaching the windows. The proper conservation technique is correct thinning of each tree in such a way that its natural appearance is not lost.[2] If Tree Preservation Orders have been placed on trees which are reducing daylight to houses, the planning authority should co-operate by allowing this kind of thinning to take place under its guidance.

A particular charm of many urban landscapes is the occasion offered by entering small enclosed spaces from the large scale streets and buildings and busy life of the city; the churchyards of many city churches are examples. If the gravestones are removed, there is more room for the passive recreational activities of strolling and browsing, but it can be argued that, apart from family connections still extant for some graves, the gravestones are essential to this particular landscape and have historical significance. The other side of this argument is that for some time in the early history of the church, hardly any gravestones were present so that the landscape was uncluttered. But a sympathetic re-design can retain the churchyard atmosphere whilst providing a much needed amenity for people today. (See also Chapter Two).

A not dissimilar situation is the 'Georgian Square' where the original concept in many examples was that the interior green space should be available only to the residents; bearing in mind the limited and passive recreational use of these 'common gardens' when the squares were first occupied, a particular kind of green landscape sometimes evolved with trees, groups of shrubs and grass. This kind of landscape will not accomodate the large number of people seeking short-term recreation now that many of these squares have lost their residential use and the green space is made accessible to the public, and a more open landscape is sought. Again, a skilful and sympathetic re-design is necessary to open out the ground space in such a way that the result seen from outside the boundaries is not too different from the original concept. There are similar kinds of problems with the conservation of the earlier 19th-century public parks, which must now qualify as historic landscapes. But the larger size allows more scope for retaining some areas exactly as planned while adapting other areas to today's recreational uses. If these parks do not attract people today with the decline of the Sunday afternoon parade because they have not been adapted to current recreational needs, it is not difficult to foresee that local authorities will be unwilling to spend much money on their upkeep.

There are several matters which act against the conservation of the tree population of a city, and I use the word 'conservation' and not 'preservation' advisedly because trees have a limited life, and there must be a continuous tree planting programme in order to keep a stable tree population for the future. Short term measures like Tree Preservation Orders to prevent removal, tree surgery, correct thinning and pruning are necessary, and the regular maintenance items of ensuring a supply of water and fertilizer, but unless there is a replacement programme, these will in time be insufficient to maintain the tree population. Changed circumstances in cities since the older trees were first planted have brought the bad effects of smoke, petrol and diesel fumes upon the leaves of trees, while the demands of wide carriageways, over-head lighting and underground services have interfered with the roots and branches, and now the elm trees are threatened or have already died. Looking after trees can be an expensive business, and in view of the value of trees to the landscape we all see and enjoy, whether the trees are growing on public or private land, some kind of national advisory or care service for trees would be preferable to the present position where some trees are well cared for and others left to look after themselves. Vandalism is another hazard to which young trees especially are vulnerable, and the attempts various authorities have made to combat it are well documented and need not be repeated.[3]

The future of canals in cities seems to be not just a matter of conserving them, but of adapting them to new uses, unless they can be brought back to their original use as a transportation system for industry. There are successful examples where people have found the canal environment in cities very suitable for residential development, and its waterscape is always an attraction for locating restaurants, public houses and craft shops.[4] But to realize the full potential of canals in cities, the surroundings require equal attention in conservation terms as the canals and their artefacts.

There are many transient elements of the urban landscape which reflect changing fashions and taste, such as the colour of the public transport buses and street furniture. It would be asking too much if these were subject to too much standardization and control, but the hope is that the conservation of both the rural and urban landscapes may rank as a subject in formal education at all levels in order that informed opinion may arise over conservation issues. There is planning control of advertisements and this is right because they rank in a visual sense as part of the building to which they are attached, but it would be a happy situation if public taste and interest were such that the control of advertisements was unnecessary.

[1] The Bibliography gives some useful references on the subject of the preservation of buildings.
[2] There are now several good references to the correct way to prune and thin trees, and a selection is given in the Bibliography.
[3] E.g. Central Policy of Review Staff, *Vandalism* (HMSO: London, 1978) and Hackett, B., *Thwarting the Vandal by Design*, Redland Record, No 37 (1974), pp. 18–20. *Landscape Development of Steep Slopes* (Oriel Press: Newcastle upon Tyne, 1977).
[4] White, P., *Waterway Environment Handbook*, (Loose leaf manual design guide). First ed. 1972, British Waterways Board, The Locks, Hillmorton, nr. Rugby.

Chapter 8

Comprehensive conservation

The surroundings of a building or a tree which warrant preservation are often just as important to the appearance of the building or tree as the objects themselves. This fact was emphasized by the International Council of Monuments and Sites in a declaration in 1964 issued in Venice which states that the concept of an historic monument embraces not only the single architectural work, but also the urban or rural setting. There are also many examples where a building or a tree in a rural or urban landscape is not in itself sufficiently unique or of high quality to justify preservation, but, taken together with other buildings or trees of similar quality, the group as a whole is worth preserving as a conservation area. In order to provide for group preservation appropriate legislation has been introduced in some countries, but in Britain with the emphasis on protecting the built environment, although the setting of a town or village, and views in and out of them, can be added to a conservation area.

The idea of conservation of a comprehensive area of landscape is inherent in National Parks, National Forest Parks, Areas of Outstanding Natural Beauty, Green Belts, and to a lesser extent in Country Parks; Heritage Coasts also rank in this respect, having been identified and suggested for inclusion in the structure and local plans. Each one of these landscapes depends upon the whole, rather than the particular, for its upgrading as special quality landscape. The question may well be asked why the procedure for scheduling Areas of Outstanding Natural Beauty is not all that is needed for conserving landscapes in the countryside, and indeed this is a suitable procedure when the landscape is entirely 'green', even if it is not entirely 'natural', which is the position in many ANOBs with landscapes developed by man. There are many areas where some buildings or artefacts of interest in the countryside are set in a green landscape which by itself is not of outstanding beauty, but where the landscape *in toto* justifies conservation. There is also a suggestion with the ANOB procedure that the landscape, having 'natural' beauty, can look after itself; there are, however, many 'humanized landscapes' which require conservation rather than merely preservation, which infers that a conservation area procedure is the right one. At the present time, the statutory conservation areas under British legislation are intended for the conservation of groups of buildings, rather than 'green' landscapes. If the intention was extended to the latter, and bearing in mind the land use aspect of so much of the 'green' landscape for agriculture and forestry, a grading system for conservation areas would seem appropriate — perhaps on the following lines:

1. Areas of genuine natural beauty, compared with

8.1 *The map showing the boundaries of the conservation area designated by the Staffordshire County Planning Authority in connection with the village of Enville which lies within the area of the old Kinver Forest. The conservation area includes the village and the Hall, and the area is characterized by abundant tree and hedge planting which help to link buildings otherwise appearing in places to be scattered. The historical interest of the area was an important reason for the designation, and the parkland landscape was regarded as important for its role as the setting for the Hall. The grounds of the Hall were developed in the 18th and 19th centuries, almost certainly by Shenstone and in part by Sanderson Miller. (Courtesy of the Staffordshire County Planning Department)*

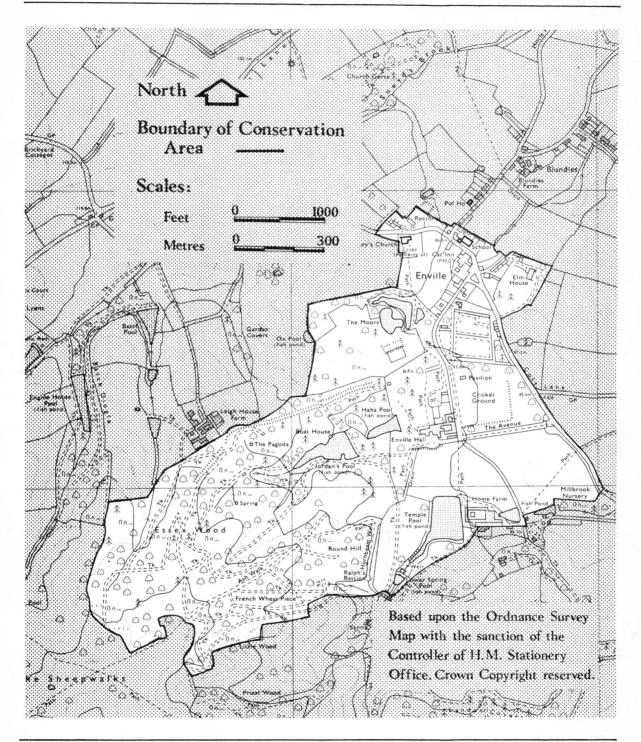

North

Boundary of Conservation Area ——

Scales:

Feet   0 ———— 1000

Metres 0 ———— 300

Based upon the Ordnance Survey Map with the sanction of the Controller of H.M. Stationery Office. Crown Copyright reserved.

humanized landscapes, parallel with the existing Sites of Special Scientific Interest, and with strictly controlled access.

2. Areas of outstanding humanized landscape (e.g. historic landscapes), with recreational access and a presumption against development.

3. Areas with strict planning control of development, such as proposals for hedgerow removal and the external appearance of proposed buildings.

Merely designating a conservation area is only half the battle because, to be effective, it must be followed by continuous action to maintain its status, and immediate action to repair damage and the results of fair wear and tear; also, effective control and advice must always be available to ensure that any new works are in character with the area. In Britain, the degree to which the objectives of a conservation area are carried into effect is strengthened when the influence of an advisory committee, set up for this purpose, is added to the authority of the statutory planning committee and its planning department and is in operation for the statutory conservation areas of many local authorities which are intended for the conservation of groups of buildings rather than for 'green' landscapes. The expectation of those concerned for the environment is that there should be a high standard of planning control in these areas. The standard of control is illustrated by the present legal requirement that a proposal to fell or carry out some lesser operation to a tree which is not subject to a Tree Preservation Order in a conservation area must be notified to the planning authority at least six weeks before the date when the notifier wishes to carry out the operation – this procedure is in order that the planning authority may be able to take preventive action.

The strength of a conservation area advisory committee lies in three principles of membership, if observed. The inclusion of perhaps half its members from outside the statutory planning committee would bring a concentration of interest on conservation. If these 'outside' members are drawn from amenity societies, professional bodies involved in environmental matters, and other interests of a community nature, there will be both expertise and an impartial view of proposals having rateable value attraction for the local authority. And often the influence of a committee, of whom many of its members receive no monetary recompense, even for expenses, is considerable. Because of the weight of responsible opinion generated by such a committee, some of the problems

of divided responsibility within a local authority are overcome. For example, work to the roads in a conservation area in Britain is the responsibility of a highways committee, and lack of co-operation between planning and highway departments can lead to design details for the roads and paving being at variance with the character of the buildings. A conservation area advisory committee of the kind indicated can bridge the gap between the two standards and speak with authority although without any power of compulsion.

The reference to the importance of the surroundings to a building or a tree also applies to a conservation area as a whole because a boundary drawn tightly around the buildings and 'green' landscape, qualifying for conservation on historic or appearance grounds, may not ensure adequate control of a zone beyond the tight boundary which allows views into and out of a conservation area. The solution is to extend the tight boundary or to have a zone beyond it where the spaces favourable to these views are maintained, but with the normal planning control elsewhere in the zone. With a conservation area based mainly upon 'green' landscape, a zone of control beyond it may prove necessary in order to safeguard the vegetation. Industrial pollution from outside the conservation area can be disastrous to vegetation; a problem which has occurred in Japan is the drying up of a remote source of water supplying the pools and streams of an historic garden in a conservation area through urban development at the source.

The designation of a conservation area may in time attract more visitors to it, and thus introduce a traffic problem; this possibility needs to be taken into account in the traffic arrangements within and even beyond the zone which was suggested outside the tight boundary of a conservation area. The Staffordshire County Council have designated a linear conservation area based upon a canal. Although largely concerned with recognizing the historical and technological significance of this monument of the Industrial Revolution, the descriptive designation document published by the Council notes that the canal passes through some of the most attractive countryside in the County. The boundaries of the conservation area are in places more widely drawn than the canal curtilage to afford a degree of protection to this surrounding landscape. Elsewhere it is intended to afford a measure of protection to the landscape setting of the canal, including both views from and to it through the formulation of appropriate local plan policies, and through the sympathetic exercise of development control powers. This particular County Council has also established several rural conservation areas based upon parkland landscapes attached to country houses of historic value and architectural merit. It is noteworthy that the purpose behind the designation was 'to afford some recognition to the importance of the landscape setting of important country houses and their historic garden monuments', and 'to afford a degree of protection to the historical interest of the landscapes themselves, either as good examples of a particular genre of landscape design, or for their importance in the oeuvre of a particular landscape designer.'[1]

The idea of a 'zone of concern' is not dissimilar to the 'zone protégé' in France which extends up to 500 metres around the scheduled and listed buildings. The idea of a conservation area has also been taken up by other countries, such as the protection afforded to areas comprising buildings, streets, trees, etc., in the Netherlands by an Ancient Monuments Act of 1961, and the 'secteurs sauvegardés' established under legislation of 1962 in France.

Drawing the boundary of a conservation area is a straight-forward task when the area is 'all of a piece', such as a rural estate comprising the house, the parkland and woodland, and which was laid out in

8.2 *A redevelopment scheme in the mediaeval part of the City of Stockholm. Development of the interior of the block over the centuries was cleared, and the space used as an attractive communal garden for the people living in the reconditioned apartments facing on to the streets which surround the block.*

accordance with a landscape plan, as often happened in Britain in the 17th to the early 19th centuries. But when an area under consideration for designation as a conservation area has many separate properties, with areas of no special interest between them, the task is not easy. Circular 23/77 of the Department of the Environment leaves the task of proposing the designation of a conservation area to the planning authority, whilst giving some general indication of what one might expect to find in such an area.[2] The following suggestion may help to decide whether the conservation area procedure is likely to be successful, compared with the Preservation Order method for individual buildings and trees: a preliminary boundary can usually be drawn around an area within which separate properties of interest for conservation occur. Within this area the land over which views of, and from, each property are possible and which provides a setting, is identified. If the lands belonging to each property and the lands concerned in the views cover most of the area within the preliminary boundary, there is a strong case for designating the whole area. But with the reverse situation, a developer's argument that planning control, aimed at overall conservation is inappropriate, might be more convincing at a public inquiry into the setting up of a proposed conservation area, and the objectives of conservation might be better achieved if Preservation Orders were applied to individual buildings and trees. At some date well into the future, views and a setting can be reinstated, but once a property of historic or architectural interest is lost, only reconstruction is possible. An alternative is to have something like the 'zone of concern' with an obligation rather than compulsion to redevelop in a manner which respects the separate properties, and to rely upon individual Preservation Orders for the separate properties.

A conservation area comprising 'green' landscape would pose fewer problems for a planning authority over development applications than an urban area, because its visual unity, compared with the complex appearance of most streets and buildings, implies a decisive 'yes or no'. A planning authority has a difficult decision to make when a proposed development out of character with an urban conservation area is proposed for a site where it will not be in the public view. A walled garden of historic importance and not in the public view does, however, justify preservation because of its inherent interest. These are examples of the variety of situations which may arise in a conservation area, and do not justify a standard decision.

There are a few areas where the conservation policy could be of the 'museum' kind, but most areas have to accommodate people in the way of housing and commerce, and problems inevitably arise from the higher standard of living now required when the fabric belongs to a past age. Two examples of a satisfactory outcome are the clearance of the centres of blocks of historic development in the old city of Stockholm to make common gardens for the remodelled interior elevations of the buildings fronting on to the surrounding streets, and the letting of old buildings in Fredrikstad, Norway, to artists who make designs for products to be manufactured elsewhere in factories.

It is sad to reflect that if there was adequate planning control over demolition and alteration to the worthwhile examples of town and village fabric, and adequate planning powers to foster good and sympathetic design standards for replacement and infilling, the need for conservation areas in towns and villages would hardly arise. The same might be said for large areas of landscape in the countryside, but the point has to be made that landscape is a single being, with each constituent element dependent upon the other, compared with the many different elements in towns and villages which are dependent one upon the other only in economic and visual terms and not for their source of life. The test surely is whether the present safeguards for landscape areas in the form of National Parks, National Forest Parks, Areas of Outstanding Natural Beauty, Country Parks, Green Belts, Heritage Coasts and Sites of Special Scientific Interest can be applied to all the landscapes which ought to have assistance in the form of conservation measures and financial aid. There are still many gaps when the statutory areas were mapped in relation to the nation's landscapes of quality and historic interest.

[1] As stated by the County Planning Officer, Staffordshire County Council.
[2] Department of the Environment, Circular 23/77, *Historic Buildings and Conservation Areas – Policy and Procedure* (HMSO: London, 1977).

Chapter 9

Continuing conservation

There is no point in attempting to refer to all the many construction, earthworks and planting operations likely to be needed in repair and restoration work, and in the continuous process of maintaining landscapes which have been scheduled for conservation. These operations are mostly those associated with civil engineering, building architecture, and landscape design, and information about them is given in the standard technical works; some useful references, with the emphasis on conservation, are given in the Bibliography. Nevertheless, there are some general principles which merit discussion.

In many countries, the planning authorities are in the fore-front of conservation because they can establish the basis and, in some cases, require a scheduled property to be looked after, although there are many loopholes in this kind of surveillance. Land use planning can safeguard the surroundings and contribute to the limitation of traffic, although it may take a long time to accomplish an overall improvement from the control of land use. Speedier action which a planning authority can take in Britain is in the preservation of trees and buildings, and in the conditions attached to the granting of planning permissions; the possibilities for this kind of action are greater in the towns than in the countryside (see Chapter Five).

Planning control, with the conditions it can impose upon the use of, and further changes to, landscape, does not overcome the problem of financing conservation. Before any repair, restoration or continuing maintenance works can be put in hand, the necessary finance has to be available; heavy taxation and rising costs limit what private owners can do in these respects, and the grants that are available are very

limited (see Chapter Ten). In agriculture and forestry, the economic and labour situations present difficulties to both the private and public landowners, while some areas of rural landscape have been changed or are at risk because of proposed mining and reservoir projects, and these warrant special care when designing the restoration of, or adjustment works to, the landscape. Other examples of change and risk come from a combination of urban expansion and the motor car which have brought transitory and commuter populations far into the countryside and surburban populations into the rural landscape around the towns. Reliance has to be placed upon the planning authorities and the Central Government to safeguard within their powers those landscapes which have been singled out for conservation through scheduling, for example, as Areas of Outstanding Natural Beauty, and they find it difficult to act unless there is public support. An example of their difficulty when public support comes from both sides is the pressure put upon planning departments by the urban population to allow more caravan sites in the countryside and by the opposition from amenity societies and some country dwellers; even a compromise decision between a few large sites and scattered groups of three or four

Overleaf

9.1 *The necessity for felling diseased trees is demonstrated in this illustration of the woodlands at Petworth Park, West Sussex. But without a plan of selective felling and replanting from the early stages of a woodland, gaps inevitably are left until new planting has developed sufficiently to fill the gaps. There is also likely to be a temporary change to the groundflora whilst the gaps remain open. The National Trust has now taken over the task of conserving the landscape at Petworth.*

caravans over a large area of countryside is difficult to determine.

Byelaws framed by local authorities within the relevant Acts of Parliament and regulations by landowners can be effective as practical measures for conserving landscape (see Chapter Six); for example, by controlling the number and type of boats allowed on an inland water, the stirring up of mud is kept to a degree which does not reduce the illumination below that needed by many aquatic plants. Byelaws are difficult to enforce when deterioration of the landscape occurs as a result of some distant operation such as the draining of plant nutrients from the fertilizer spread on fields some distance away which eventually reaches a lake through ditches and streams and interferes with the quality of the water. Or when the erosion of a bank of a stream leads to the silting-up of a reed swamp at the entrance to a lake so that it becomes an alder or willow carr with a consequent change in wildlife. Byelaws and regulations are usually local in their effect, and, to control the kind of situation in these examples, some authority operating over the same territory that nature operates is needed. The rationalization in England of Water Authorities into large regions is a step in this direction.

The amount and manner in which water is present in and on the land is critical to the kind of landscape — lack of it produces a 'desert', and a high water table produces marshland. It follows that the water level has to be maintained as a continuing factor in conservation, and this can be difficult to control when the sources of water are so spread out and under the control of many ownerships. If drainage channels are cut in the slopes of peat moorland in order to achieve a lower water table for planting tree seedlings, there is a danger of flooding in the valley below because the water from a heavy storm runs quickly down the channels instead of being absorbed in the peat and released slowly. If navigation is improved on a river by constructing a lock, the water table around the river above the lock will rise, and trees and shrubs in the vicinity will die from waterlogging, although they may eventually be succeeded by plants which accept the new conditions. A recent example of maintaining the status quo of a landscape justifying conservation was the disapproval in 1978 by the Minister of Agriculture, Fisheries and Food of a 900 acre drainage scheme at the Wild Brooks, near Arundel in Sussex; the evidence of the Nature Conservancy Council and others included the fact that lowering the water table would lead to drastic changes in the flora and fauna of a type of landscape now becoming a rarity.

Modern agricultural practice calls for efficient drainage systems which will control the water table at the optimum levels needed for various crops, but this is often achieved without concern for the lands upstream and downstream. By straightening stream channels, keeping them cleared of trees and shrubs on the banks and introducing sluice gates, the water table can be kept at a particular level on the land in question, but in dry weather the land downstream will lack water and have too much in wet weather, and the land upstream will lack water in clement weather as a result of the increased flow. There is also the effect land drainage works of this kind will have upon the appearance of the landscape and upon the wildlife population. A watercourse management system which operates on a continuing basis, and resolves the differences between the advocates of modern agriculture and landscape conservation, is surely the answer — in the words of the Conservation and Land Drainage Working Party, 'With a sensitive approach to watercourse management conflicts should not arise and result in surrendering the character and aesthetic value of the landscape.'[1]

When the conservation policy leads to the reconstruction of a landscape which has few, if any, remains left, some people condemn the action as spurious or covering up the little that is genuine. Nevertheless, reconstruction has educational value and also, as at Williamsburg in the USA, recreational value. With many buildings, there is no denying the fact that many famous examples of buildings and artefacts, surviving the next one thousand years, will have been completely re-faced through necessity, and with landscape there will have been many new generations of vegetation. The dilemma is between hoping against hope that the original can survive the centuries, and making certain that people in the future will have examples to demonstrate how their ancestors lived, and often in a more congenial environment as regards noise and appearance, though less sanitary.

One of the better ways of conserving the rural landscape is to revive old techniques of the rural industries which were responsible for the landscape being as it is. A revival over the whole countryside is not possible with today's changed social and economic state, but there are a few people who seek a simple rural life and who could be brought into a project to conserve a few areas by using the original forms of management in the manner now proposed for conservation. Setting up these people on the land would be a proper use for conservation grants, even to the extent of bridging the gap between the old and new economic situations by regular financial aid; recent television programmes have focussed on some pioneers of this particular conservation practice.

Agricultural and forestry practices are the chief activities for maintaining rural landscapes, but when a practice which produced a landscape of amenity value is no longer possible today, and it is planned to conserve this landscape, the alternative put forward by Lord Porchester for the areas of moor and heath in the Exmoor National Park is one solution:[2] grants should be made to farmers to bridge the gap between the conservation management and converting the moorland to a more profitable practice. Another suggestion was to legislate for a system of Moorland Conservation Orders, subject to the right of appeal and

public inquiry, where there would be a restriction against farming practices which would change the moorland character, and with a single compensation. With the latter suggestion, it might not always be possible to hold a farmer to the letter of the Order

9.2 *A conservation zoning plan for the Robert Allerton Park, Monticello, Illinois, USA. This was a private estate donated to the University of Illinois and is used as a recreation and conference center, also for research and teaching purposes. A Master Plan was drawn up to arrange for the various uses in a way where they would take place in sympathy with the landscape, of which this zoning plan shows the distribution of uses, and is supplemented by more detailed studies ·of the land use and conservation proposals. The explanation of the zones is as follows: Zone 1: Public park area and an example of early 20th-century landscape design. Zone 11: The education and research area. Zone 111: A transition area between the public park area and the education/research area. (Courtesy of Prof. W. Keith, University of Illinois)*

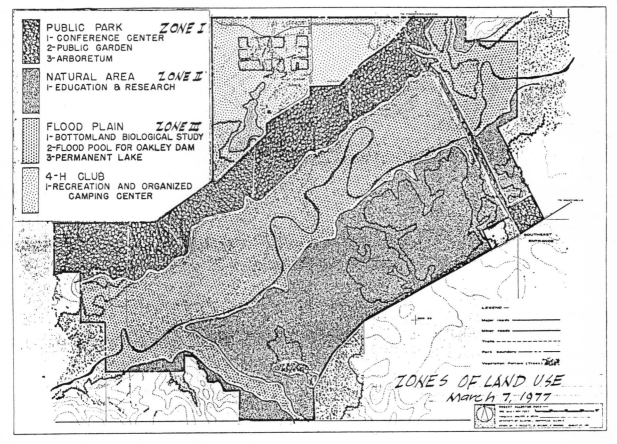

when the economic situation may be quite different in the future; there could be many reasons why a farmer is unable to maintain the degree of sheep grazing needed to keep the heathland in the traditional state.

The revival of some of the rural craft industries might encourage a revival of the practice of coppicing woodland which produces the small diameter timber used in some crafts. The traditional products may not be in demand in the 20th-century world outside the village, with the result that markets need to be found for new products from the old crafts. Adjustment of a traditional skill or practice to satisfy today's markets will often mean accepting a smaller financial return rather than introducing a new skill or practice; an example is limited selective felling of trees in a woodland, compared with the clear felling demands of the modern sawmill, in order to conserve the appearance of the landscape without any temporary changes. The dilemma of deciding whether to clear fell an avenue of trees was referred to in Chapter Five, taking Hampton Court as an example. John Workman, Advisor on Conservation and Forestry to the National Trust has suggested ways of conserving trees in avenues of different kinds.[3] If the avenue is very wide and not very long and forms the visual frame to a building, the policy should be to replace the trees here and there because the foliage will be more visually significant than the trunks of the trees. If the avenue is very narrow, then reasonable lengths could be clear felled and replanted on each side. And, if the avenue is long and the width brings the trunks of the trees into prominence, another complete avenue should be planted elsewhere to take its place. There is, of course, the possibility that planting could take place outside and parallel with the trees which would be clear felled when the outer avenue was at a stage of growth when it began to look impressive, but this would eventually lead to a temporary situation of a much wider avenue until the replanting of the original avenue had also reached an impressive stage.

There is the dilemma of the single or specimen tree and how to keep its place in the landscape. Tree surgery can prolong the life of some aged trees, but it is usually an expensive operation and likely to be reserved for trees in key positions in the appearance of the landscape.[4] The indefinite future of a tree in a key position means planting a substitute nearby, unless, after the old tree is felled, a semi-mature tree, already prepared, is planted in the same position provided the old roots can be removed. If the conservation policy is to keep intact the groundflora of a woodland, selective felling or thinning the crowns of the trees may be necessary in order that sufficient illumination reaches the ground for the groundflora to flourish. The Countryside Commission is now encouraging local authorities to apply for grants for the maintenance of trees, and the results of good care can be seen, for example, in many of London's parks. But there is also the opposite view of some nature conservationists who prefer that a tree should not be interfered with, perhaps forgetting that the tree surgery work has resulted from man's inevitable influence upon the landscape.

The countryside management procedure initiated by the Countryside Commission was referred to in Chapter Five, and under the project or management officer, conservation is a continuing process. Perhaps new legislation dealing with countryside management, either in the form of a new Act or as an amendment to the Countryside Act, could gather together the many ideas embodied in the reports and papers that have appeared in recent years on the future of agriculture and the landscape.

Continuing conservation also involves arrangements to balance the wear and tear on the landscape from recreationalists with the ability of the vegetation and soil to recover. Rivers, canals and particularly lakes do not suffer to the same extent from this wear and tear as land based areas, and there is still unrealized potential in the waters of most countries for relieving the pressure on the land, although this could alter the ecology of some wetlands.

[1] Cf Chapter One note 1.
[2] Lord Porchester, *Exmoor Study* (HMSO: London, 1977).
[3] Cf Chapter Three, note 3.
[4] British Standards Institution, *Tree Surgery B.S.I. 3998: 1966, Recommendations for Tree Work* (BSI: London).

9.3 *The avenue of Japanese cedar trees in the Nikko National Park, Japan. The conservation policy required the protection of the tree roots alongside the road by the use of stone walling.*

Chapter 10

Enabling and paying

There was a time when landscape conservation took place without the assistance, or control, of legislation, and when the cost was met by the landowner. This was all very well when the agricultural and forestry practices matched the layout of the landscapes we now seek to conserve, and when the landowners had the money and labour available for the maintenance of the amenity landscapes. But the financial problems of landowners today with landscape justifying conservation, and the pressure upon them from land-hungry developers, has brought to the fore the need for legislation, backed up by financial assistance, to conserve as many as possible of the beautiful and historic landscapes still remaining.

In Chapter Four, the question of listing and scheduling was shown to be an essential preliminary to conservation plans, and similarly, and to be logical, legislation for conservation should require that the whole country is surveyed to ascertain those areas of landscape which fit the various categories likely to be of interest for conservation, and also those defined by the legislation; listing and scheduling ought then to follow. The survey task is not so formidable as it may at first seem, because planning authorities already have a good knowledge of the various landscapes of their areas and assistance can be available from voluntary bodies, but the decision on what should and should not be listed is more difficult.

Some special landscapes already have legislative backing which covers their identification and subsequent management, such as Areas of Outstanding Natural Beauty and Sites of Special Scientific Interest. Listing and scheduling under legislation is, in itself, a contribution to conservation, although the large areas of land and the complications of the land use activities of landscapes render the example of the restrictions placed on owners of listed and scheduled buildings inappropriate for landscape conservation; some other safeguards would be required for listing and scheduling landscapes which would take into account the circumstances referred to, particularly the arrangements for regular maintenance and periodic replanting.

The National Trust adopts various methods for conservation of its landscapes: 'In some cases gardens remain under the influence and continue in the tradition of their donors; sometimes they are managed by Local Committees, while in other cases local experts with special knowledge are asked to supervise. . . at all costs the Trust seeks to avoid uniformity . . . to seek out and maintain the character of each individual garden is so important that the sacrifice of some administrative ease is willingly made.'[1] And with respect to the Trust's woodlands: 'The management . . . . is in the hands of the Regional Agents, working through Regional Foresters, head foresters or head woodmen depending on the area and the amount of work involved. The regional staff can call on the Trust's Advisor on Conservation and Woodlands and his assistants.'[2] Concerning much larger areas of land, there are the local authority committees for the National Parks and the Countryside with some members appointed by the local authority from among its councillors and others appointed by the Central Government; also, there is the new consortium of representatives from interested bodies, to deal with the conservation of the Broads, which has a limited period in which to demonstrate that it is capable of doing the job.

The National Trust's view that administrative uniformity is inappropriate for landscape conservation is a wise one and this, combined with the Countryside Commission's watching brief on the Broads' consortium, suggest that several kinds of management of landscape are possible under a central body, and the choice for a particular landscape should be dependent upon the ownership, the kind of landscape, the land uses involved, and the grant aid situation. Responsibility to a central body when it makes grants should include approval of the kind of management and a review by the central body at suitable intervals of the effectiveness of the management. The particular landscape uses and interests of each area are essential to its management and if these interests are properly taken into account, the members of a management body are likely to be drawn from landscape architects, farmers, foresters, and, in some cases, water and land drainage engineers and wildlife organizations. These interests should also be represented on the central body. In France, an Administrative Unit of the Ministry of Cultural Affairs is the central body handling conservation, including scheduling the most important examples, with listing as the second priority; in addition to buildings, gardens and the immediate surroundings of historic monuments can be scheduled and listed, and when scheduled, no repairs or alterations may be carried out without Ministry approval. In Britain, the Countryside Commission, the Ministry of Agriculture and Fisheries, the Nature Conservancy Council and the Ancient Monuments Board each act as a central body for the conservation of those landscapes which come within their terms of reference; but, apart from tree preservation and the stricter planning control of 'green' landscape in a conservation area and Green Belts, reliance has to be placed on the normal planning process to prevent amenity landscapes being swallowed up by development, and there is no statutory listing procedure for these landscapes despite the obvious need to conserve such important elements of the nation's heritage. It is, of course, questionable whether all the selected examples of the types of landscape, classified in Chapter One, should be placed on one statutory list under one central body because under the existing system, where several bodies have their own statutory duties, the specialist interests may show more concern than one comprehensive body — at the very least, amenity landscapes, other than those for which provision is already

made, should have statutory recognition.

By placing a landscape on a list with the objective of conservation, some weight is given to an objection at a public inquiry against a change into some other form; also, listing sometimes makes the landowner realize the value of the landscape in his possession and care. The most effective legal device is something akin to a Building or Tree Preservation Order, but the problem with landscape, which occurs to a lesser extent with trees, is the continuous maintenance compared with the task of putting a building into a sound state with the prospect of little maintenance for many years — a Landscape Preservation Order would have legal loopholes because it is not possible to keep everything alive indefinitely.

The Environmental Impact Statement required under the National Environmental Policy Act, 1970, in the USA, is another method of achieving the objectives in the listing and scheduling of landscapes when they are at risk from some proposed change. Under this Act a statement must be prepared on a proposed major Federal development which assesses the consequences of carrying out the proposal. It could be said that the right of people to raise objections to a planning application for development gives them the opportunity to suggest what the consequences might be, but this places a financial, time consuming and the 'seeking of expertise' burden upon the objector which is usually beyond his capability. To be of value, an Environmental Impact Statement should be prepared by impartial experts or is technically thorough and accurate, and its findings taken into consideration in a democratic process of decision making. British legislation relating to public bodies goes some way towards the aims of an Environmental Impact Statement; for example, Section 22 of the Water Act, 1973, upholds 'the desirability . . . of protecting buildings and other objects of architectural, archaeological or historic interest and shall take into account any effect which the proposals would have on the beauty of, or amenity in, any rural or urban area or on such flora, fauna, features, buildings or objects'. This is a step in the right direction, but 'shall take into account any effect'

Overleaf

10.1 *The Ishibutai Tomb, Iwaido, Japan. An example of an ancient monument in a landscape setting, the monument itself being more of a landscape element than a human artefact.*

is not the same as making an Environmental Impact Statement.

At the very least, the advantage of listing, followed hopefully by scheduling, for conservation is that the landowner has to hold back on felling, clearing, demolition or alteration until his proposals have been fully investigated. The 'early warning' proposal referred to in Chapter Five for the countryside could be adopted also for amenity landscapes, but does not have the weight of authority given by statutory listing and scheduling.

In Britain, the legislation for conserving landscape is provided in several Acts of Parliament, which relate to different activities and circumstances. Section II of the Countryside Act, 1968, places a duty upon public bodies to have regard to the desirability of conserving the natural beauty and amenity of the countryside — not a very strong provision, but one under which a challenge could be made at a public inquiry to demonstrate how this regard was taken into account.[3] Section 22 of the Water Act, 1973, mentioned pre-

viously, is more specific, 'shall take into account' being a little more definite than 'having regard to'. Planning legislation, dating from the 1947 Act, in its over-riding control of land, except under agriculture, forestry and the Crown, can control the change of use of land, but not the maintenance of existing amenity landscapes, but some planning authorities have defined maintenance operations in some planning approvals for new developments. Also, under planning legislation, Tree Preservation Orders can be made, while under the Town and Country Planning Act, 1971, supplemented by the Town and Country Planning Amenities Act, 1974, any work proposed to a tree

10.2 *A plan, prepared by the Norfolk County Planning Department, to show how the environment of the homestead of a farm could be improved with the addition of shelter belt planting which also helps to relate the farm buildings to the surrounding countryside. The proposals are shown by a broken line. Planting of this kind is likely to meet with approval for grant aid from the Countryside Commission. (Courtesy of the Norfolk County Planning Department)*

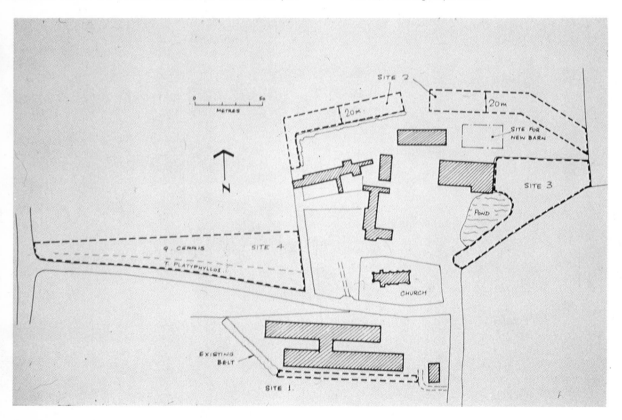

in a conservation area which can be established under this Act, must be notified to the planning authority not less than six weeks before it is proposed to carry out the work, thus giving time for action to be taken. Under Section 277 of the Town and Country Planning Act, 1971, planning authorities can designate areas of special architectural or historic interest as conservation areas, and whilst conservation area legislation in Britain places the emphasis on areas with buildings, it can hardly pass unnoticed that the Act states 'areas of special architectural *or* historic interest' (Author's italics), and there are many areas of green landscape, without any buildings, which are of historic interest; the Civic Amenities Act, 1967, included a similar provision. Under Section 52 of the 1971 Act, a landowner and a planning authority can make an agreement to restrict or regulate the development or use of land belonging to the owner, in the same way that a restrictive covenant operates; this Section could be used to conserve an area of landscape, and the agreement can include provisions for its conservation. Conservation issues seem to be implied in Circular 75/76 of the Department of the Environment (Development involving Agricultural Land) in the reference to planning authorities having regard to ecological and amenity factors in relation to agricultural land and development when preparing local plans.

The legislation for areas within which stricter planning control is envisaged, such as the National Parks, Areas of Outstanding Natural Beauty, and Sites of Special Scientific Interest, is in the National Parks and Access to the Countryside Act, 1949, extended by the Countryside Act, 1968, and in the Town and Country Planning Acts. Circular 108/77 of the Department of the Environment advised planning authorities to include nature conservation in their planning proposals and decisions on planning applications,[4] and they have the services of the Nature Conservancy Council, the County Trusts for Nature Conservation and voluntary societies available for advice. There is also the Town and Country Planning (Landscape Areas Special Development) Order, 1950, which is now applied under Section 24 of the Town and Country Planning Act, 1971; this enables a planning authority in certain specified local authority areas of beautiful landscape to control the design and external appearance of agricultural and forestry buildings when applications for development are made.

Despite this mass of legislation in Britain which can

be used to further landscape conservation, landscapes, whose main interest is historical, lack adequate legal protection until there is a statutory listing and scheduling procedure, except for examples which exist only as 'remains', and these can be conserved by the Ancient Monuments Board. Why do we have to wait until little remains of historic landscape before legislation recognizes the need to conserve historic landscapes? Ancient monuments can be protected under the Fields Monuments Act, 1972, by a payment to the occupier of land to compensate him for avoiding interference with a monument when there is a danger that it will be injured in the course of agricultural or forestry operations. The Commons Registration Act, 1965, was designed to regularize the conservation of the historic commons, but the dispute procedure had 26,000 cases still to settle in 1978, and there are weaknesses in the legislation over such matters as public access, management and improvement.

Footpaths and bridleways are integral parts of the landscape, and their conservation is aided by the definitive maps required by the National Parks and Access to the Countryside Act, 1949, which requires that public rights of way in the form of footpaths and bridleways be kept free from obstruction and not permanently disturbed. Public footpaths are maintained by the local authorities who have to supervise the duty of landowners to repair stiles and gates across rights of way on their lands. Voluntary bodies, like the Commons, Open Spaces, and Footpaths Society, the Rights of Way Society, and the Ramblers' Association keep watchful eyes on public rights of way.

Some species of flora and fauna of the landscape are protected under the Conservation of Wild Creatures and Wild Plants Act, 1975, but not when they are affected by the work of public bodies carried out in accordance with their statutory duties. There are also many Acts dating from the 19th century for the protection of birds and fish.

Historic landscapes fare better under legislation

Overleaf

10.3 *One of the entries submitted for the 1979 Hedgerow Campaign Competition run by the Northumberland County Planning Department. This County's Campaign published a **Hedgerow Guide**, one thousand copies being distributed to farmers, parish and district councils, libraries, etc. In the adjoining Co. Durham, a botanical and historical survey of hedgerows was carried out in 1978 and is published by the Durham County Conservation Trust under the title **Hedges in Durham County**, by A. J. Bailey. (Courtesy of the Northumberland County Planning Department)*

which enables grants to be made for their restoration and conservation, instead of legislation which is only protective. The Historic Buildings and Ancient Monuments Act, 1953, amended by Section 12 of the Town and Country Amenities Act, 1974, enables grants to be made under Section 4 for the upkeep of a garden or other land of outstanding historic interest, and it does not have to be attached to a building of similar interest. And grants may be made towards the upkeep of gardens associated with buildings of architectural or historic interest, whether or not listed, by local authorities under the Local Authorities (Historic Buildings) Act, 1962, amended by the Town and Country Amenities Act, 1974. The recent economic situation has, however, led the Historic Buildings Council to advise restraint on work to open spaces, except when a project can be organized under a 'job creation' scheme.

The Countryside Commission has the main responsibility for making grants with respect to rural landscapes of different kinds, including National Parks, Country Parks, countryside management projects, and experimental work, such as the demonstration farms (see Chapter Five); the Forestry Commission's work in managing some of the older forests is also an example of the financing of conservation, together with its grants under the dedication and small woods schemes. The conservation of woodland is to some extent achieved by Section 9 of the Forestry Act, 1967, which requires the owner to obtain a felling licence from the Forestry Commission to fell growing trees, with some exceptions as to the quantity in any three months and trees of small size or trees in gardens and public open spaces, etc.

The fact that landscape conservation is a continuing process has been mentioned several times; thus, financial aid should continue beyond an initial grant for restoration and replanting, unless these works enable the landscape to be put in a state where it can attract sufficient income for its own maintenance. The key to a solution seems to lie in complete tax exemption in respect of the land, both annually and at the owner's death, which is how the National Trust in England and the New York State Departments in the USA through the National Heritage Trust manage to keep their heads above water, aided by admission fees, subscriptions and bequests. In Britain, Section 77 (1) (b) of the Finance Act, 1976, allows exemption from Capital Transfer Tax, on the advice of the Countryside Commissions for England and Wales and for Scotland, when landowners are prepared to enter into management undertakings to conserve 'the scene'.

It is becoming a general rule that when substantial grants are made from public funds for restoration, preservation and conservation, the property should be open to the public, and when the owner remains in residence, an arrangement whereby access is limited to certain days and times, or to certain months, and to some parts of a building or some areas of a landscape, is a fair compromise. Where a lesser grant towards the cost of restoring or replanting a particular part of a building or landscape supplements the owner's contribution, it would not be unreasonable to take the view that the owner has played his part in safeguarding something of the nation's heritage for the future, usually against the severe odds of inflation, and the burden of making the property accessible to the public should not be made a condition of this lesser kind of grant. We should not overlook the fact that private ownership of a property, especially over several generations, is not easily given over to public ownership in order that public money may be made available for conservation; during these generations the private ownership will have ploughed in money for conservation and also have contributed increasingly large amounts to the Exchequer through taxation and death duties. At the same time, the public likes to see where its money goes. Unfortunately, every now and then conservation becomes a party political issue when safeguarding many of the good things in a nation's heritage ought to be divorced from party politics.

Professor Shigeto Tsuru of Japan has suggested a National Defence Fund for Cultural Treasures, to be financed partly by tax revenue and partly by a special bond issue; in making this suggestion, he made the point, when comparing expenditure for military defence with expenditure on cultural defence, that the latter was 'in the nature of maintenance and investment for the future . . . including defending from deterioration the positive assets of the land such as historic landscape and places of natural beauty'.[5] The National Land Fund, set up in Britain in 1946, is not dissimilar to Professor Tsuru's suggestion, but its diversion for other purposes has led to a proposal that it should be in the hands of trustees, who would ensure it was used for conserving the national heritage, and given a new name – the National Heritage Fund. Landscape conservation is a national responsibility with international significance recognized by fourteen countries, including Britain, in the Ramsar Convention adopted in 1971, whereby each signatory country was required to promote a number of general conservation measures, and to designate suitable areas as wetlands of international importance.[6] Our hope is that the recommendations of UNESCO and ICOMOS (see Chapter One) and other organizations on the conservation of landscape will not pass unheeded.

[1] *The National Trust and Gardens*, leaflet (The National Trust; London, 1973).

[2] *The National Trust and Woodlands, ibid.* (1976).

[3] E.g. The Opencast Coal Act, 1958, and the Pipelines Act, 1963.

[4] Department of the Environment, *Nature Conservation and Planning*, Circular 108/77 (HMSO; London, 1977).

[5] Professor Shigeto Tsuru, *Who is to bear the burden of safeguarding historic landscape*, International Symposium of Experts for the Safeguarding of Historic Landscape (Tokyo, 1977).

[6] *Convention on Wetlands of International Importance especially as Waterfowl Habitats*, Cmnd. 6465, Treaty series No. 34 (1976) (HMSO: London, 1976).

Bibliography

General

Advisory Council for Agriculture and Horticulture, *Agriculture and the Countryside (The Strutt Report)*. Ministry of Agriculture, Fisheries and Food, Pinner, 1978

Barber, D., *Farming and Wildlife*. Royal Society for the Protection of Birds, London, 1970

Countryside Commission, *Areas of Outstanding Natural Beauty – a Discussion Paper*. HMSO, London, 1978
Grants for Amenity Tree Planting and Management. HMSO, London 1977
Grants to Local Authorities for Countryside Management Projects. HMSO, London 1978
Grants to Local Authorities and other Public Bodies for Conservation and Recreation in the Countryside. HMSO, London 1974
Local Authority Countryside Management Projects. HMSO, London 1978
Grants to Private Individuals and Bodies for Conservation and Recreation in the Countryside. HMSO, London 1974
Grants for Recreation Footpath in the Countryside. HMSO, London, 1976

Countryside Review Committee, *Conservation and the Countryside Heritage — a Discussion Paper*, HMSO, London, 1979
The Countryside – Problems and Policies. HMSO, London 1976
Food Production in the Countryside — a Discussion Paper, HMSO, London, 1978
Leisure and the Countryside — a Discussion Paper, HMSO, London, 1977

Davidson, J., and Lloyd, R., eds., *Conservation and Agriculture*. John Wiley and Sons Ltd, Chichester, 1978

Department of the Environment, *Report of the National Park Policies Review Committee, (Sandford Report)*. HMSO, London, 1974

Dobby, A., *Conservation and Planning*. Hutchinson, London, 1978

Executive Committee, *Proceedings of the International Symposium of Experts for the Safeguarding of Historic Landscape*. ISHL, Tokyo, 1977

Gruffydd, J. St Bodfan, *Protecting Historic Landscapes*. College of Art and Design, Cheltenham, 1977

International Council of Monuments and Sites, *Proceedings of the First International Symposium on Protection and Restoration of Historical Gardens*. ICOMS, Paris, 1971

Miles, C. W. N., and Seabrooke, W., *Recreational Land Management*. E. & F. N. Spon Ltd, London, 1977

Porchester, Lord, *Exmoor Study*. HMSO, London, 1977

Steele, R. C., *Wildlife Conservation in Woodlands,* Forestry Commission Booklet No. 29, HMSO, London, 1972

Tanner, M. F., *The Potential of Towpaths as Waterside Footpaths*. Water Space Amenity Commission, London, 1977

Various Authors, *'Managing the Countryside'*, The Planner, Vol.65, No. 1, London, 1979

Westmacott, R., and Worthington T., *New Agricultural Landscapes*. HMSO., London, 1974.

Wright S. E., 'Rural Conservation', *Landscape Design*, Nos. 124/5, London, 1978/9.

Technical

Beazley, E., *Design for Recreation*. Faber and Faber, London, 1969

Bridgemann, P. H., *Tree Surgery – a Complete Guide*. David and Charles, Newton Abbot, 1976

British Standards Institution, *Tree Surgery B.S.I. 3998*. BSI, London, 1966

Brooks, A., *Hedging*. British Trust for Conservation Volunteers, London, 1975
Walling, ibid, 1977
Waterways and Wetlands. 1976

Brown, G. E., *The Pruning of Trees, Shrubs and Conifers*. Faber and Faber, London, 1972

Central Policy of Review Staff, *Vandalism*. HMSO, London, 1978

Department of the Environment, *Trees and Forestry – Circular 36/78*. HMSO, London, 1978

Hackett, B., *Landscape Development of Steep Slopes*. Oriel Press, Newcastle upon Tyne, 1972
Landscape Reclamation Practice. IPC Science and Technology Press, Guildford, 1977

Institute of Advanced Architectural Studies, *Architectural Conservation* – a Bibliography. IAAS., York, 1977

Ministry of Agriculture, Fisheries and Food, *Farm and Estate Hedges – Fixed Equipment of the Farm Series No. 11*. MAFF, Pinner

Nature Conservancy Council, *Hedges and Shelter Belts*. NCC, London, 1976
The Conservation of Limestone Pavements. Ibid, 1974
Lowland Farming. Ibid, 1977
Ponds and Ditches. NCC, Ibid, 1973
Sand Dune Conservation and Recreation. Ibid, 1974
Tree Planting and Wildlife Conservation. NCC, London, 1974
Nature Conservation an Introduction. Ibid, 1978

Property Services Agency, *Landscape – Guide to Sources of Information*. PSA, Library, Croydon, 1978

Smith, J. F., *A Critical Bibliography of Building Construction*. Mansell, London, 1978

Streeter D., *'Gulley Restoration on Box Hill'*. Countryside Recreation Review, Vol. 2, Countryside Commission, Cheltenham, 1977

Thomas, G. S., *'The Restoration of Gardens'*, Landscape Design, No. 125, London, 1979

Walshe, P., and Westlake, C., *Tree Guards – Management — and Design Note 6*, Countryside Commission, Cheltenham, 1977

Water Space Amenity Commission, *Conservation and Land Drainage Guidelines*. WSAC., London, 1978

White, P., *Waterway Environment Handbook,* (Loose leaf manual design guide), First Ed. 1972, British Waterways Board, The Locks, Hillmorton, Nr. Rugby.

Legislation and circulars

Town & Country Planning Act, 1947

National Parks and Acess to the Countryside Act, 1949, Coast Protection Act, 1949

Town and Country Planning (Landscape Areas Special Development) Order, 1950

Historic Buildings and Ancient Monuments Act, 1953, Section 4 (amended by Section 12 of the *Town and Country Planning Amendment Act, 1974)*

Local Authorities (Historic Buildings) Act, 1962 (amended by the *Town and Country Planning (Amendment) Act, 1972)*

Commons Registration Act, 1965

Civic Amenities Act, 1967, Section 1

National Parks and Access to the Countryside Act, 1949

Amenity Lands Act (Northern Ireland), 1965

Forestry Act, 1967, Section 9

Countryside Act, 1967, Section 66

Countryside (Scotland) Act, 1967

Countryside Act, 1968, Section 11

Town and Country Planning Act, 1971, Sections 24, 28, 52, 277

Fields Monuments Act, 1972, Section 1

Town and Country Planning (Amendment) Act, 1972

Water Act, 1973, Section 22

Town and Country Planning Amenities Act, 1974, Section 12

Wild Creatures and Wild Plants Act, 1975

Finance Act, 1976, Section 77(1) (b)

Department of the Environment, Circular 75/76, *Development involving Agricultural Land*

Department of the Environment, Circular 4/76, *Report of the National Park Policies Review Committee*

Department of the Environment, Circular 23/77, *Historic Buildings and Conservation Areas, Policy and Procedure*

Department of the Environment, Circular 36/78, *Trees and Forestry*

Department of the Environment, Circular 108/77, *Nature Conservation and Planning*

Index

Rice field 33
Rights of Way Society 101
Ringstrasse 82
Royal Forestry Society 40
Rural conservation area 87
Rural landscape 18

S

Safeguarding 14, 23
Scree area 31
Secteurs sauvegardés 87
Shadows estate 72
Shenandoah National Park 30
Sites of Special Scientific Interest 40, 58, 86, 88, 96
Social Science Research Council 18
Specimen tree 94
Staffordshire County Council 86
Stockholm 88
Stonehenge 16

T

Taxation 22, 40, 65, 68, 89, 104

Technical advancement 9
Tree preservation 35, 48, 55, 58, 82, 83, 86, 97, 100
Tsuru, Prof. Shigeto 104

U

UNESCO 13, 14, 40, 44, 105
University of Manchester 41
Upton Castle 35, 48
Urban gardens 35
Urban landscape 75, 78

V

Vandalism 83
Village 48
Voluntary conservation 59, 61

W

Water Act 97, 100

Water Authority 92
Water Space Amenity Commission 9, 18
Water table 18, 92
Waterways Recovery Group 61
Wear and tear 31, 94
Wibberley, Prof. G. 26
Wild Brooks 92
Wild landscape 30
Wildlife 35, 55
Williamsburg 22, 35, 92
Wordsworth, W. 37
Workman, J. 35, 94

Y

York 79

Z

Zone of concern 87, 88
Zone protégé 87